The Battles OF
Connecticut Farms AND Springfield
1780

SMALL BATTLES

Mark Edward Lender and James Kirby Martin, Series Editors

The Battles OF Connecticut Farms AND Springfield
1780

EDWARD G. LENGEL

SMALL BATTLES

WESTHOLME
Yardley

Westholme Publishing, LLC
904 Edgewood Road
Yardley, Pennsylvania 19067
Visit our Web site at www.westholmepublishing.com

ISBN: 978-1-59416-338-8
Also available as an eBook.

Printed in the United States of America.

To Bruce and Lynne Venter
And Sally the Beagle

Contents

List of Maps

A gallery of illustrations follows page 48

Series Editors' Introduction

WE ALL HAVE HEARD and likely read about the big battles of the American Revolution. Names like Trenton, Saratoga, and Yorktown resonate in our ears. But what about all the smaller battles that took place by the hundreds, often fought away from but related to the bigger battles? It is the contention of this series that these smaller actions, too often ignored, had as much impact, if not more, in shaping the outcomes of the American War of Independence.

These engagements were most often fought at the grassroots level. They did not directly involve His Majesty's professional forces under the likes of Generals William Howe, John Burgoyne, and Henry Clinton, or Continentals under Generals George Washington, Nathanael Greene, or Horatio Gates for that matter. Such smaller battles involved local forces, such as patriot militia and partisan bands of Loyalists, or at times Native Americans mostly, but not always, fighting on the British side.

Quite often the big names were not there in such smaller-scale combat. Private Joseph Plumb Martin, writing in his classic memoir, recalled his fighting at Forts Mifflin and Mercer during November 1777. He and his comrades were trying to block British war and supply vessels moving up the Delaware River from reaching the king's troops under Sir William Howe, who had captured Philadelphia. Had they prevailed and cut off this obvious supply route, Howe might well have had to abandon the city. No, they did not succeed. Superior British firepower finally defeated these courageous American fighters.

What bothered Martin, besides so many good soldiers being seriously wounded or killed, was not the failed but valiant effort to cut off Howe's primary supply line. Rather, writing thirty years later, what particularly irked him was that "there has been but little notice taken of" this critical action. Martin was sure he knew why: "The reason of which is, there was no Washington, Putnam, or Wayne there. . . . Such circumstances and such troops generally get but little notice taken of them, do what they will. Great men get great praise, little men, nothing."

While Martin's blunt lament is unusual in the literature of the Revolution, the circumstances he described and complained of are actually fairly obvious. Although often brutal, the smaller engagements too frequently have received short shrift in popular narratives about the conflict. Nor have the consequences of these various actions been carefully studied in relation to the bigger battles and the outcomes of the War of Independence more generally. Small battles accounted for more than a lion's share of the actual combat that occurred during the American Revolution. The purpose of this series is to shine a bright new light on these smaller engagements while also getting to know those lesser persons who participated in them and likewise grapple with the broader consequences and greater meaning of these actions on local, regional, and nation-making levels.

In the end, a more complete understanding of the Revolutionary War's big picture will emerge from the small battles volumes that make up this series. If, as recent scholarship tells us, local history "allows us to peer deep into past societies and to see their very DNA," the Small Battles Series will do the same for the American War of Independence.

Thus we are happy to commend your attention to this exciting new volume, *The Battles of Connecticut Farms and Springfield 1780,*

SERIES EDITORS' INTRODUCTION

by Edward G. Lengel. Lengel, an established authority on the War of Independence and the former editor of *The Papers of George Washington*, has offered an incisive view of these engagements that drew in New Jersey militia, a major contingent of Continental regulars, Loyalist troops, Hessians, and a strong deployment of redcoats. The campaign of roughly two weeks demonstrated the impact of the war on regional civilians as well as a maturing patriot mastery of compound warfare (the coordination of regulars with irregular combatants). Lengel sorts out what happened and why, and along the way he fills in a number of gaps in the existing historical record and corrects errors from previous accounts. His *Battles of Connecticut Farms and Springfield 1780* is now the most telling account we have of this brief but important campaign.

Mark Edward Lender
James Kirby Martin

Overleaf: "A sketch of the northern parts of New Jersey," by John Hills, 1780. Many places discussed in this narrative can be seen on this detail of Hills's map: moving from west to east, Morristown, Chatham, the Short Hills, Springfield (labeled within the Short Hills), Vauxhall (to the north of Springfield), Connecticut Farms, Elizabeth Town, Bergen Point, and New York City. (*Library of Congress*)

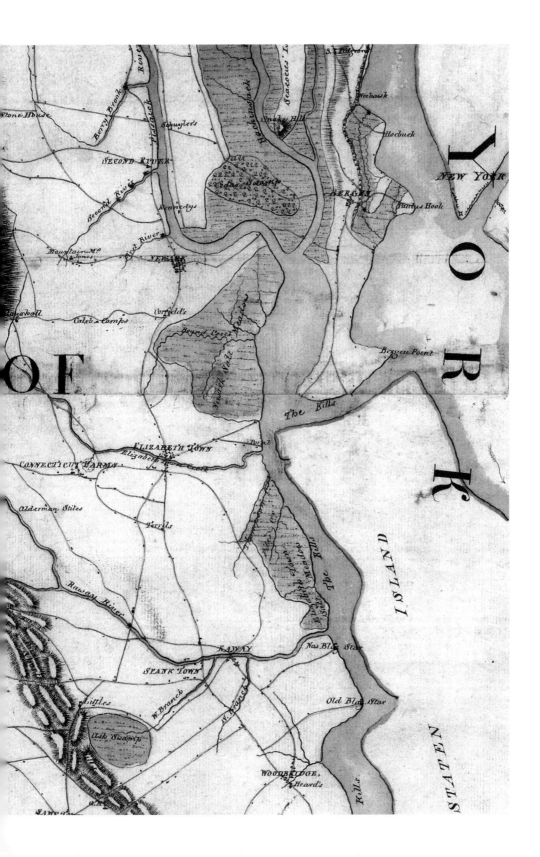

Introduction

GEORGE WASHINGTON AND HIS SOLDIERS had never been colder. Morristown, New Jersey, was a brutal encampment, occurring over the 1779–1780 winter season that remains the worst in the recorded history of the United States. Howling wind driving monstrous snowdrifts, crackling cold—Morristown had it all. Washington, though, worried most about administrative and logistical issues as he paced the floor in the Jacob Ford mansion, while his ten thousand or so men shivered down in and around Jockey Hollow. Two years earlier at Valley Forge, army supply administration had collapsed, bringing the troops to the verge of starvation and forcing the commander in chief to strive mightily to overhaul the system. Now that administration had collapsed again, and in the worst possible circumstances. As so often during the war, he found himself working to rebuild what he had thought already accomplished.

Even so, much had changed. The Continental army had come a long way since its travails in the campaigns of 1775–1776. From the war's triumphant early moments following the British evacuation of Boston in March 1776, the revolution's fortunes had taken a steep dive following the catastrophic defeat on Long Island in August and retreat from Manhattan in September. That autumn, Washington led his dissolving army out of New York and across New Jersey, pursued by enemy forces that seemed to take delight in committing atrocities against American civilians. Though undoubtedly exaggerated in some cases, these atrocities—including widespread looting and rape—helped to galvanize opponents to British rule, but they also set a precedent for ruthless conduct on both sides in the campaigns that followed. Washington's brilliant turnaround at Trenton and Princeton in December and January 1776–1777 forced British lieutenant general Sir William Howe to pull back most of his forces to New Brunswick, abandoning his conquests in New Jersey as Washington established winter camp in Middlebrook. Several months later, though, everything collapsed again.

Seventeen seventy-seven was a miserable year. After trying and failing to entice Washington out of Middlebrook that spring, Howe launched an amphibious expedition through the Chesapeake Bay. Landing at Head of Elk, Maryland, Howe's troops skirmished with Brigadier General William Maxwell's light infantry at Cooch's Bridge, Delaware, on September 3, and eight days later attacked Washington's main army at Chadds Ford on Brandywine Creek. While troops under General Wilhelm von Knyphausen drove Maxwell's men back to the ford and demonstrated against Washington's main army, Howe led the major effort against the American right flank. The result was a crushing defeat for the Continental army, although Major General Nathanael Greene averted total catastrophe in a firm rearguard action. On September 26, the British captured Philadelphia. Washington's attempt at a Trenton-style surprise attack failed at the Battle of Germantown on October 4. Then, in a drawn-out campaign, Washington lost control of the Delaware River forts he had hoped to use to cut off waterborne supplies to the city.

Although Lieutenant General John Burgoyne's surrender at Saratoga on October 17 helped convince France to enter the war as an ally of the United States, it did nothing to boost Washington's reputation or the morale of the miserable troops under his command. In December, the army moved into winter quarters at Valley Forge, where Washington faced accusations of mismanagement and having lost the army. Some worked quietly or even called openly for his dismissal. He not only weathered the storm but gained the army's allegiance through his example of careful management and hard work. French intervention caused the British army, now under the command of General Henry Clinton, to abandon Philadelphia and march across New Jersey to Sandy Hook, where the troops boarded ships for New York. At the Battle of Monmouth Court House on June 28, Washington fought the British to a standstill partly by virtue of his personal command; afterward, he successfully spun the battle as a victory. By fall 1778, Washington had attained a firm and permanent grip on the Continental army.[1]

The war's character also changed. French intervention led to new strategic priorities on both sides. For a time, the British focused on the West Indies; but in 1779–1780, North America again became a major theater, as Clinton maintained his base in New York City while initiating a campaign to roll up the South, beginning with Georgia and South Carolina. Throughout this period, Washington and the Americans sought opportunities to collaborate with the French in inflicting a severe and possibly decisive defeat on the British. The first allied efforts, at Rhode Island in 1778 and Savannah in 1779, had not gone well; but hopefully the third time would be the charm. Despite discussion and abortive preparations for a joint invasion of Canada, Washington pinned his hopes on New York City.

Washington's preoccupation with New York City dovetailed with a strategic vision that he had maintained since the war's beginning. The United States, he firmly believed, did not have time on its side. As an astute businessman and combat veteran, Washington recognized better than most the challenges the young country would face in financing a protracted war effort. Weak government and an emerging postcolonial economy practically guaranteed financial disarray that would severely limit the Continental army's operational options. Worse, Washington justifiably doubted the American public's ability to endure crushing economic hardship. It was vital to end the war as quickly as possible.[2]

The Continental army's development reflected the commander in chief's strategic vision. Where other Americans preferred a militia-based army designed to handle local military emergencies and disrupt Loyalist efforts to reassert control, Washington set about designing an armed force that would be capable of both defensive and offensive operations. Led by competent officers operating within a clearly defined military hierarchy, backed by efficient army administration and logistics, well equipped and well trained, the Continental army should be able to withstand blows and deliver them too.

A key component of the army's development, and one Washington emphasized from the very beginning, was the establishment of a strong system of internal and external intelligence, with a view to adequate appraisal, assessment, and strategic planning. Put simply, Washington and his officers should enjoy at all times a clear view of their own military assets and capabilities as well as those of their enemy, enabling them to take decisive action at any moment. This had been a major problem during the first three years of the war, leaving the Americans incapable of effectively parrying enemy blows or of seizing military opportunities. Instead of abandoning his efforts, though, Washington had redoubled them, in large part by preparing the army under his command for an all-out assault on New York City in conjunction with French land and naval forces. This was the reason for his hard work since 1778, not just in army administration but in military intelligence and espionage. The army must be poised to strike hard at the right moment.[3]

Thanks to these efforts, by 1780 the Continental army had become, despite its winter travails, more precisely an instrument of war than ever before. Imperfections certainly remained. Poor supply administration and the nation's worsening economic problems induced shortages, weak recruitment, and often low morale. Crucially, however, by 1780 Washington could "see" his army clearly and use it almost at will. He enjoyed an accurate knowledge not just of the forces under his immediate command but of detachments and other assets. Also, thanks to his strong communications skills, he maintained a much better sense of regional political and military realities than ever. Unlike in previous years, he could communicate quickly and easily with governors and local officials, and understand militia dispositions and capabilities instead of just having to wonder about them. His command was more centralized and his leadership more confident.

Washington also could count on his officers like never before. By 1780, most of the liabilities had been weeded out—at least in the areas under his immediate command. The men on his staff and with higher-level field commands were quality officers whom he knew and understood—as they, in turn, understood the commander in chief's preferences without having to be told. They worked together well. Generals Nathanael Greene, Henry Knox, Friedrich von Steuben, and Anthony Wayne were all prime examples of this, as were men like General Maxwell, Colonel Elias Dayton, and Major Henry Lee Jr. This heightened military efficiency and improved command proved decisively important in the events of June 1780.

The British army, meanwhile, had in some respects been moving in the opposite direction. Never again would America see a British force akin to the one Howe had wielded in 1776–1777. No more—though Washington didn't know it—the grand schemes to sever New England and reassert royal control over the middle colonies. As an empire, Great Britain was no closer to defeat in 1780 than it had been five years earlier. British land and naval forces had on the whole maintained the upper hand over France in the war's various theaters; and the country's economic staying power—as the events of 1792–1815 would prove—remained strong. Though somewhat shaken by their inability to subdue the rebels so far, King George III and his ministers in London remained determined to prosecute the war to a victorious conclusion. And although grave deficiencies existed in British strategic planning and military administration, they were nothing that a man or men of ability—a Pitt the Elder or Pitt the Younger—might have been able to solve.

The prime causes of British military weakness were threefold and interrelated. First, the logistical challenges of conducting a global conflict had had a profoundly adverse impact on the British army in North America. Since 1778, the campaign in the West Indies and Lord George Germain's interest in conducting a southern campaign—which Clinton resisted but could not stop—diverted scarce resources of men and supplies from the prime base in New York City. In 1779, this had reduced Clinton to a frustrating state of near-inactivity that sapped his morale and the confidence of his officers and men in his leadership.[4]

Second, while Washington better understood and could wield—even if he didn't always like—the militia, the British had increasingly lost confidence in the Loyalists. Indeed, the feelings went both ways. Although individual Loyalist units such as Lieutenant Colonel John Graves Simcoe's Queen's Rangers performed well overall, others had done poorly and recruitment lagged. Much of this was due to successful repression by the Congress and its minions, which British leaders poorly understood. Where Howe had at least hoped for Loyalist uprisings in the mid-Atlantic in 1777, three years later Clinton had come to accept that no such possibility beckoned, at least in the near future. The best he was willing to hope for from the Americans in the short term was apathy or exhaustion, rather than active support. This stance enraged Loyalist leaders ensconced in New York City, who remained certain that many Americans would be willing to support the king if strong efforts were made to reach them.

The third and most important deficiency in the king's North American arms was the failing morale of its leaders. Clinton, a talented soldier who had arrived in America with Howe and Burgoyne in 1775 and taken over from Howe in 1778, had no stomach for command; at least, not at this time and place. By the beginning of 1780, he had already attempted to resign multiple times. And although the expedition against Charleston, South Carolina, upon which he embarked in December 1779 ended in victory six months later, he embarked upon the expedition only reluctantly and derived little satisfaction from it.[5]

Clinton's lack of enthusiasm for his job, which may have stemmed from psychological causes, was infectious. While he sailed to Charleston, his deputy, Lieutenant General Wilhelm von Knyphausen, took over the garrison in New York City. This capable officer, whom we shall come to know well in the course of this study, performed effectively in combat under Howe but was not to excel under his successor. Like many others, he chafed under Clinton's pessimism and perceived inactivity; in council and on the battlefield, in consequence, he alternated strangely between hot-tempered aggressiveness and quick despair.

The same could be said of the British, German, and American field officers and soldiers serving under Howe's command. They were still perfectly willing to fight, and head for head remained tactically superior to Washington's Continentals. In battle, though, their hard-hitting aggressiveness tended by this point of the war to dissolve quickly into loss of focus, followed by angry disgust. Sometimes they vented these feelings on each other and sometimes on the Americans; in any event, their military ventures frequently lost cohesion over time. Such are the consequences of poor leadership.

Even as Washington and his soldiers struggled through the hardships at Morristown in winter and spring 1780, then, they were in the process of gaining an irreversible ascendancy over their opponents. These advantages were all but invisible on the surface. The Continental army in spring 1780 seemed on the verge of collapse, scarred as it was by ongoing scarcities in food, pay, and other necessities. Angry and even mutinous as the soldiers became, though, they retained two assets essential to victory: trust in Washington and the officers under his command, and confidence in their ability to contest the field of battle. This gave them a strength and constancy in adversity that Clinton's troops increasingly lacked. It began at the top and unfolded in June 1780 upon the battlefields of Connecticut Farms and Springfield, New Jersey.

ONE

Armageddon in View

THE PORT OF BREST, on the tip of the Brittany Peninsula on the west coast of France, teemed with ships in spring 1780. After many weeks of preparations, undertaken well in the open and observed by British spies, French troops began boarding troop transports in April. On May 2, the transports weighed anchor and set sail for North America, shepherded by warships. Sailing with them in command of the land force was Marshal Jean-Baptiste Donatien de Vimeur, comte de Rochambeau. His mission: to cooperate with American forces in a decisive campaign against the British in North America.

Across the ocean in British-occupied New York City, Wilhelm von Knyphausen knew about the preparations for Rochambeau's expedition. Although he wouldn't receive news of the expedition's departure for many weeks, he had to be prepared against the possibility that it might already be at sea. Born in Lower Saxony in Germany in 1716, he had served in the army of Frederick the Great of Prussia, being wounded as a major at the Battle of Bergen in 1759 and eventually becoming a lieutenant general in

1775. Sent to America in 1776, Knyphausen demonstrated efficiency and aggressiveness that earned him considerable distinction. He carried out the assault on Fort Washington, on Manhattan Island, in November 1776 with great bravado, dismantling the fortifications with his bare hands; the fort was subsequently renamed in his honor. For this and his conduct during the subsequent pursuit of Washington's army across New Jersey, he was awarded command of German auxiliaries in America in 1777. Knyphausen justified the honor in his conduct at the Battle of Brandywine in September 1777, and the Battle of Monmouth in June 1778.

Knyphausen's aggressive instincts remained in evidence after he took command of the British army garrison in New York City following Clinton's departure for Charleston in December 1779. New Jersey paid the price for Knyphausen's bellicosity. Troops under his command launched significant raids into the state in January, February, and March 1780—including a quixotic effort to capture the American commander in chief—and many smaller incursions. These were short but bloody affairs that often ended in significant damage to civilians and their property. The primary purpose of these raids was to keep the rebels off balance and give hope to local Loyalists, but they also served notice to Knyphausen's men that they had better be prepared for action under his command. Though close-lipped and stern, Knyphausen was efficient, fair, and highly respected by his troops. His inclination for battle made them like him even more.[1]

News of the French expedition, and uncertainty over when Clinton would return and whether in victory or defeat, enforced some degree of caution on Knyphausen. In April he ordered his troops to reinforce their already formidable defenses around New York City against the possibility that the French would achieve naval superiority offshore. To this end, they buttressed defenses on Bayard's Hill north of the city and sank hulks in Sandy Hook Channel to obstruct passage there. These were no more than healthy precautions, however. Knyphausen's instincts drove him always to seek offensive action. He soon had his opportunity.[2]

THE BRITISH DEFENSIVE PREPARATIONS, about which his spies informed him promptly, told Washington that the enemy was worried about the possibility for which he hoped: the arrival of the French fleet off New York. Major General the Marquis de Lafayette, just returned from France, arrived in Morristown on May 10 to help the Americans plan for cooperation with Rochambeau's approaching forces. Neither he nor Washington, though, knew for certain when or where the fleet would appear. Off Charleston, to relieve that beleaguered bastion from Clinton's siege? Or in New England, perhaps at Rhode Island? Even if the fleet did appear off New York, the Americans could only hope that Rochambeau would be both competent and ready to fight. Whatever the case, Washington was determined that the troops under his command would be prepared. His determination arose from desperation.

The Morristown winter had been bad enough. At least the spring weather was warmer. In May, however, a perfect storm of crises emerged that threatened to demolish the army and possibly, Washington and others believed, sink the Revolution. From all appearances, the Continental army looked weaker at that moment than it had been for years. The three-year enlistments established in 1777—so welcome at the time after two successive years of annual enlistments—expired in 1780, and few of the soldiers showed any disposition to remain in service. Their field officers hardly set an example of durability. For a variety of reasons, not least pay arrearages and economic dislocation, an epidemic of officer resignations swept through the army from March to May.[3]

Rebuilding wasn't easy. On May 15, Washington wrote to Massachusetts politician James Bowdoin, complaining that he commanded merely "the Skeleton of an Army" thanks to a "pernicious system" by which states offered bounties to men who signed on to even short militia enlistments. This undermined his attempts to rebuild a Continental army that could keep the field through to the end of the war. Worse, poor conditions in the army relative to provision shortages and pay arrearages were contributing to a rise in desertion, which British and Loyalist agents did their best to encourage. Many deserters were caught in the act and sentenced to death. On May 26, Washington employed his favorite method of issuing pardons to several condemned men as they stood on the scaffold. This effort to combine fear and mercy had intangible effects, however; the desertions continued, thanks in part to fairly easy escape routes from Morristown to New York City.[4]

Other pressures were external. Although Charleston fell to the British on May 12, word of the disaster did not arrive at Morristown until the following month. In the meantime, Washington—who in mid-April had sent the Maryland Division to reinforce the doomed city—endured constant pressure to send more. Major Henry "Light Horse Harry" Lee Jr. already was slated to depart for the South with his legion, but fortuitous instinct led Washington to cancel this movement on May 20—in time to stop the legion's cavalry, if not the infantry. Farther north, incursions by Indians and Loyalists on the New York frontier—recurring in the aftermath of Major General John Sullivan's expedition of the previous year—led Washington to detach Brigadier General James Clinton's New York Brigade of about 1,100 men plus an artillery company and send it to Albany at the end of May. He could ill afford any further reduction.[5]

The Continental army's woes were symptomatic of larger problems that seemed irremediable. The army's rickety funding system—if it deserved the name—that had functioned more or less since 1775 had by the beginning of 1780 fallen completely to pieces. Unable to raise revenue effectively due to lack of federal authority, and facing an empty treasury, Congress had over the preceding winter implemented a state-based funding process to provide for the army's needs. States, however, looked to their own priorities first before supporting Congress, with the result that Washington's commissaries lacked funds not just to pay officers and men but to pay for basic necessities, especially food. Major

General Nathanael Greene, serving as quartermaster general since Valley Forge, increasingly found himself at his wits' end to secure supplies. Toward the end of May, Washington's troops in New Jersey and elsewhere were reduced to near-starvation rations and had no meat for several days at a time. The results were grim.

The army's predicament was no secret. Washington shared it with many correspondents, including a congressional camp committee convened to confer with the general at headquarters that summed it all up in a circular to the state governors on May 25. The committee declared:

> That the Army was five months pay in arrears, that it has Seldom or ever, since it took this cantonement, had more than Six days provision in advance—That at present it is without meat, and has been on half, and on quarter allowance for some days past. That the Commissaries cannot give any assurances of doing more than bearly subsisting the Troops from day to day—That even then they apprehend a want of meat will frequently prevail; That the Army . . . is destitute of forage for the few horses which indespensible necessity has required, should be maintaind in Camp—That it will require several Thousand horses to move the Army so as to promise any affectual operation from it—That the Sick in Hospitals have not a sufficiency of those articles necessary for their comfort . . . That as every department of the Army is without money, and not even the shadow of Credit left, consequently no article however necessary can be procured—That the Transportation even of the inadequate supply of flour, forage, and other articles hitherto furnished by the states is at a stand—That very few of the recruits required by the act of Congress of the 9th of February last have arrived—That from information received there is no prospect that any considerable number will timely engage in the service on Volentary inlistmt—That by the expiration of the terms for which men were engaged, Deaths and Desertions, the Army is so greatly reduced, that it does not afford a probable prospect of its acting with any degree of efficacy in merely defensive operations—That the patience of the

soldiery who have endured every degree of conceivable hardship, and borne it with fortitude, and perseverance, beyond
the expecttation of the most sanguine, is on the point of being
exhausted—That a spirit of discontent is encouraged by the
arts of the enemy, whose emissaries hold up in printed papers
distributed among the soldiery the most flattering prospects
and promises to induce them to desert their colours.

British and Loyalist agents must have read this admission of
weakness with profound interest.[6]

That same day, the army's sad state became apparent to all. By
this time Washington's men had gone ten days without meat, sub-
sisting on what flour, occasional vegetables, and a few odds and
ends could provide. Troops of two regiments of the 1st Connecticut Brigade, under acting commandant Colonel Return Jonathan
Meigs, expressed their frustration by getting in a squabble with a
hot-tempered adjutant at morning roll call. As the adjutant
stalked off, the troops began forming in a mutinous parade.
Quick thinking by their officers blocked the men from seizing
arms from a nearby weapons hut, but Meigs was injured in the
process. Colonel Walter Stewart, a well-liked officer, came over
from the 1st Pennsylvania Brigade to settle down the Connecticut
men and succeeded in dispersing them. The Board of War was
able to secure an emergency supply of cattle for Morristown at
the end of the month. Tensions remained high, however, thanks
in part to printed exhortations to desertion that the British managed to slip into camp; according to Washington, they had "a considerable effect."[7]

Money was on Washington's mind. The want of it had nearly
brought the American cause to ruin. What if the war continued
much longer? Confiding on May 28 in a letter to Pennsylvania
Supreme Executive Council president Joseph Reed, the commander in chief summarized America's financial and supply
problems and then looked to the longer view. "In modern Wars
the longest purse must chiefly determine the event," he wrote.
Great Britain's advantage in this respect was well-nigh insupera-
ble. "Though the [British] Government is deeply in debt & of

course poor," he continued, "the nation is rich and their riches afford a fund wch will not be easily exhausted. Besides, their system of public credit is such that it is capable of greater exertions than that of any other nation—Speculatists have been a long time foretelling its downfall, but we see no Symptoms of the catastrophe being very near. I am perswaded it will at least last out the War [and] that ample means will be found to prosecute the war with the greatest vigor."

But shouldn't the support of France and Spain outweigh British riches and allow the Americans to hold out indefinitely? Washington was not so sanguine. With profound perception and foresight, he continued, "I am well informed—if the War continues another Campaign [the French] will be obliged to have recourse to the taxes usual in time of War which are very heavy—and which the people of France are not in condition to indure for any duration. When this necessity commences France makes war on ruinous terms; and England from her individual wealth will find much greater facility in supplying her exigencies." As for Spain, "Commerce and industry are the best means of a Nation; both which are wanting to her—I am told her treasury is far from being so well filled as we have flattered ourselves—She [is] also much divided on the propriety of the War—there is a strong party against it." Time, in other words, was not on the allies' side.

Washington concluded with a shocking admission that "the circumstances of our allies as well as our own call for peace; to obtain which we must make one great effort this Campaign. . . . If we do our duty we may even hope to make the campaign decisive on this Continent. But we must do our duty in earnest—or disgrace & ruin will attend us." The "one great effort" to be undertaken to stave off total, imminent defeat was the conquest of New York City.[8]

Washington's focus on New York City did not emerge from any feelings of fondness for the place—he had been happy to see it burn in 1776. Rather, it was the most significant British possession within reach. He recognized the formidable nature of the city's defenses and knew that so long as the British maintained mastery of the seas in the vicinity, he had no chance of taking or holding the place. Since the French entered the conflict in 1778, however, he had recognized the possibility that America's new allies might achieve at least temporary naval superiority at one spot and simultaneously provide troops to collaborate with American land forces in wiping out a major British garrison. With a French fleet now on the way, the opportunity seemed imminent.

"It appears to me in the present situation of the enemy at New York," Washington wrote to Lafayette on May 16, "that it ought to be our first object to reduce that post and that it is of the utmost importance not to lose a moment in repairing to that place." For much of May, then, the commander in chief worked to scrape together all available supplies and manpower in preparation for an immediate attack on New York, when and if the French fleet arrived offshore. Estimating that the British had 17,500 men available in the city, Washington hoped to muster a force of about 40,000 men: just over two to one odds, far less than what most military leaders recognized as necessary in any such enterprise against a well-entrenched position.[9]

That Washington was willing to countenance such odds at a time when he couldn't even muster the resources to feed and equip his men under arms is a measure of his desperation. He fully recognized, moreover, that if the assault failed, his army would be destroyed and the alliance shattered, leading to absolute ruin. Failure, this allegedly Fabian warrior told the congressional committee on May 25, "instead of rescuing us from the embarrassments we experience & from the danger with which we are threatned will in all probability, precipitate our ruin. Drained and Weakned as we already are, the exertions we shall make, though they may be too imperfect to secure success, will at any rate be such as to leave us in a state of relaxation and debility, from which it will be difficult if not impracticable to recover. The Country exhausted—The People dispirited—the consequence & reputation of these States in Europe sunk—Our friends chagrined & discouraged—our Enemies deriving new credit, new confidence, new resources." Victory was the only option. The alternative was certain defeat and the end of the Revolution.[10]

MANY GENERALS IN SUCH AN APOCALYPTIC MINDSET, bordering on obsession, might well have neglected routine matters and standard defensive precautions. Washington had a powerful military mind capable of keeping many matters in view, but he was human after all. Fortunately—in view of what was to come—the Continental army posts in eastern New Jersey were vital to his larger plans and thus difficult to overlook. In December 1779, he sent Brigadier General Samuel Holden Parsons's two Connecticut Brigades (formerly Israel Putnam's division) to take post east of Springfield, New Jersey. Their purpose, Washington specified, was to gather and protect supplies; protect well-disposed civilians; prevent Loyalists from communicating and trading with the enemy; and gather intelligence on enemy troops movements in and around New York City. This latter duty was particularly close to Washington's heart and would become more so as the spring progressed. The detachment's mission was not so much to protect Morristown—where Washington appears to have felt fairly secure—as to lay the groundwork for a future attack on the city.

Parsons still had to be careful, however. He was not, the commander in chief emphasized, to post any significant forces at Newark, Elizabethtown, Amboy, or anywhere close to the shore, for fear that the enemy might surprise and destroy them in a quick movement. Rather, he was to maintain his primary force at a point more or less equidistant from these so he could move quickly and easily in any emergency. Washington exhorted Parsons to seek counsel with Brigadier General William Maxwell, commanding the New Jersey Brigade, because of his intimate knowledge of the country.[11]

The Connecticut troops remained on post for the next several months, carrying out Washington's orders efficiently. Parsons became ill, however, and by spring his troops had become severely worn down. On April 17, Parsons's replacement, Brigadier General Jedediah Huntington, wrote to Washington, complaining that "the Duty is at present as hard as in the most active Parts of a Campaign" and admitting that his command was so weakened it was unlikely to be able to prevent an enemy incursion even "with a Number much inferior to ours." On May 13, therefore, Washington dispatched Maxwell and his brigade, consisting of the 1st, 2nd, and 3rd New Jersey Regiments and Colonel Oliver Spencer's Additional Continental Regiment, to relieve the beleaguered Connecticut troops at this important post.[12]

Maxwell is one of the war's least known and most intriguing generals. He and Washington likely had known each other for more than twenty years, since they had served together during the Braddock expedition in 1755. A Scots-Irishman who had arrived in America in 1747 and settled in New Jersey, Maxwell became colonel of the 2nd New Jersey Regiment in 1775 and fought at the Battle of Three Rivers early the following year. Washington found him most useful in New Jersey, however, where his local knowledge was invaluable. During the winter campaign of 1776–1777, now-Brigadier General Maxwell remained in New Jersey, raising troops, protecting supplies, and commanding small, mixed forces of continentals and militia in a series of largely successful small-scale encounters with enemy detachments.

Washington, who seems to have viewed the 1776–1777 campaign as put-up-or-shut-up time for a number of his field and general officers, took Maxwell's measure during this period. The result was that he placed Maxwell, who had been put at the head of the New Jersey Brigade after its formation in May 1777, in command of an approximately eight-hundred-man corps of light infantry temporarily assembled for service that summer. It was in this capacity that Maxwell first encountered Knyphausen in battle. On September 3, Maxwell's light infantry, serving as screening forces, conducted a tough and respectable fighting withdrawal against Knyphausen's advance column in the Battle of Cooch's Bridge, Delaware. On September 11, he faced Knyphausen again, delaying the German's direct approach to Chadds Ford before a smart flanking maneuver forced their direct retreat.

Like most Continental army officers, Maxwell had his opponents. A hard-driving officer who enjoyed his liquor and pushed
hard for seniority and command, he alienated more than a few
of his fellow officers, especially those of junior rank. During the
Valley Forge winter, he, like several other officers, was accused
and acquitted of incapacitating intoxication on the field of battle.
The criticism persisted over the months that followed. Washington, though, continued to find "Scotch Willie" useful in an irregular role, although it is probably no coincidence that he never
asked Maxwell to command troops in a set-piece battle.

Maxwell continued to serve honorably after the light infantry
was disbanded, and he returned to command the New Jersey
Brigade. Among other things, his brigade harassed General
Henry Clinton's retreating forces during the Monmouth Court
House campaign of June 1778. Maxwell remained on post in New
Jersey for most of the following two years, except for summer
1779, when he accompanied and served honorably in Sullivan's
campaign against Loyalists and hostile elements of the Iroquois
Confederacy in upstate New York. His relations with the officers
commanding the regiments in the New Jersey Brigade were shaky
at best—but then his colonels didn't get along particularly well
with each other, either. The important thing was that Washington,
who had a record of standing by troubled but talented officers
such as Maxwell and Sullivan, still valued his services.[13]

Maxwell's deployment to Elizabethtown in May 1780, then,
made perfect sense and was to prove fortuitous for Washington
and his army. Where Huntington's Connecticut continentals had
been tired and demoralized—they would mutiny less than two
weeks after returning to camp—Maxwell's Jerseymen knew their
ground. Though they too grumbled at the problems in the Continental army and suffered from shortages—they would mutiny
in 1781, after Maxwell's departure—they at least had the advantage of being close to home, with all of the psychological benefit
that entailed. Their numbers, though, were weak: about nine
hundred men in June 1780, just over half of what they had been
two years earlier.[14]

Maxwell's brigade deployed on May 14, nominally part of a division commanded by fellow Jerseyman—and another hard-drinking American of Scottish descent—Major General William Alexander, who styled himself Lord Stirling.[15] Alexander, though, played only a peripheral role in the events to come. Stationing the majority of his force at Connecticut Farms for the nonce, Maxwell sent guard detachments to Rahway, Woodbridge, and Newark, and dispatched Colonel Elias Dayton's 3rd New Jersey Regiment and Spencer's regiment, with Dayton in overall command, to Elizabethtown. At the same time, he assembled a party of field officers and staff and accompanied Alexander to Elizabethtown to scope the terrain and settle upon a permanent encampment. Washington dispatched a French engineer officer, Captain Etienne Bechet de Rochefontaine, to help select the site and lay out some simple fortifications, although his services proved unnecessary.[16]

While Maxwell fussed over the site of his permanent encampment, Colonel Dayton took point in carrying out the kind of duties Washington thought most important. Dayton, who was born (and eventually died) in Elizabethtown, was a highly competent officer who had seen action in both the French and Indian and Revolutionary Wars, including at Brandywine, Germantown, and Monmouth. Among his most exceptional talents were military intelligence and espionage. He worked with scrupulous efficiency. A few days after his posting, he uprooted a small Loyalist operation to convey American deserters and intelligence from New Jersey to Staten Island. He also reported on British ship and troop movements in and immediately around the city.

Also shortly after Dayton's move to Elizabethtown, a double agent he employed in Knyphausen's headquarters turned up some intriguing and potentially worrying information. Knyphausen's aide de camp George Beckwith expressed a particular interest in American dispositions around Morristown on his boss's behalf. How many men did Washington have under his command, Beckwith asked? Told that it was seven thousand to eight thousand and that they were low on provisions, Beckwith instructed the agent to go there and count huts and cannon to make sure; Knyphausen, he said, particularly wanted to know if Washington had more than four thousand troops. Beckwith also wanted particular details on where and how Maxwell's force was situated. It might not mean anything, but then again, it might.[17]

Supplied with intelligence such as this, Washington began to worry a good deal about Maxwell's and especially Dayton's safety. Virginia native Rev. James Caldwell, who had attended the College of New Jersey and then settled in Springfield with his wife, Hannah, and their nine children, kept the commander in chief regularly supplied with local information. He had just moved to the small settlement of Connecticut Farms and wrote to Washington from there on May 18 that he thought the American positions were fully secure. "I can't say I fear a surprise," he wrote. But Washington was not so sure. Since he couldn't leave Morristown owing to press of business, he told Alexander to take a lead in the matter, working closely with Maxwell and Rochefontaine. "You are to keep two things in view," he told the general, "a position that will cover the Country, for which the Brigade was sent down—and a proper regard to its own security either from surprise or from an open attack."[18]

But Maxwell continued to hesitate. Alexander appears to have remained distant from the decision for the brigade's encampment; and although Rochefontaine identified ground and began tracing out rudimentary fortifications, Maxwell discovered from some locals that the site chosen would become a bog in wet weather. Further consultation with the French engineer was impossible, because Washington then sent him on a mission to Rhode Island to prepare for the French expeditionary force's possible arrival there. Dissatisfied with the ground and worried about increasing food shortages for his brigade, Maxwell temporarily shifted his force on May 25 to a spot about one mile from Elizabethtown.[19]

The British thereupon forced up the tempo. Early on the morning of May 26, a detachment of about 150 to 250 men from the British 57th Regiment of Foot under Major Charles Brownlow embarked on boats at Staten Island, slipped undetected past Bergen Point (the American guard post at Elizabethtown Point had been placed against just such a possibility), and landed at Newark. The British surprised a small patrol, but one of the Americans managed to escape and raise the alarm. Knowing their time was short, the raiders worked quickly, capturing about thirty rebels—mostly civilians—and plundering their homes. Unlike the devastating British raid on the town of January 25, 1780, however, the Americans reacted so promptly that the raiders had little time to do much harm.

Captain Samuel Reading, leading a detachment of the 2nd New Jersey Regiment in small parties alongside some local militia who, Maxwell remarked, "turned out spiritedly," met the enemy just west of the town courthouse. Taking post behind fences and working their way around the British flanks, the Americans kept up a galling fire on the British until they pulled back to their boats, and followed them all the way to the water's edge. Although the British made off with their prisoners, they failed to do any major damage. Both sides took a handful of casualties, although Captain George Knox, a distinguished Continental officer who had just retired to get married and appeared on the field at the head of a Newark militia detachment, was shot in the mouth and lost part of his jaw and tongue.[20]

Although his detachments reacted well, the raid—combined with reports of a countryside filled with spies and informers, and ongoing skirmishing between militia and Loyalists in Bergen County—left Maxwell feeling distinctly nervous. "My sittuation is such that I think they cannot surprize me," he wrote to Washington on May 28, "but if they come out with a much superior force, they may move me from my Baggage & Camp equipage." That may be why he ordered Colonel Dayton to send the better part of his regiment one mile west to the main encampment, while keeping post at Elizabethtown only by rotating detachments. Dayton, however, protested to Washington that the arrangement was weak and unsafe, and the commander in chief immediately put a stop to it. Instead, he ordered Maxwell to offer equal protection to Newark and Elizabethtown (primarily to satisfy the inhabitants of the former, who were jealous of the priority being given to the latter) and more particularly to vacate the boggy ground where he was camping.

Pressed by the commander in chief, Maxwell finally selected a permanent post. Dayton's and Spencer's regiments remained at Elizabethtown, but the 1st and 2nd New Jersey Regiments moved to West Farms, a small settlement six miles northwest of Elizabethtown and three miles west of Newark. With Rochefontaine gone, there was no further discussion of building works—which in the event probably would have been pointless anyway. Small detachments at the outer posts were continued, and careful communication maintained with the local militia. Washington, still worried about the regiments at Elizabethtown, wrote to Dayton on May 31, "You should without loss of time be making your arrangements for defence, in case the Enemy should make an attempt upon you." He specified a "strong stone House" recommended by Rev. Caldwell that "might be put in a situation to receive you if attacked, and which might be defended untill a support could be brought up."[21]

THE HAMMER FELL AT THE END OF MAY. For weeks, Americans had been awaiting news of the fate of Charleston. James Rivington's loyalist *Royal Gazette* finally gave it to them in an extraordinary issue of May 29. The town, the paper announced, had fallen, and General Charles, Earl Cornwallis was already driving inland to liberate Loyal inhabitants from the "tyranny" of "usurpation." Dayton attempted to suppress the pronouncement of "lying Rivington," refusing to believe it to be true, as did many other Americans. Washington, though, recognized the signs of veracity and realistically, albeit painfully, accepted the truth of the report. Clinton, the commander in chief assumed accurately, would already be on the way back with his fleet and preparing to attack some post in the middle colonies. Washington feared it would be West Point.

It was just one more in a series of blows, settling Washington's certainty that the final crisis was at hand. On June 2 he dispatched a circular letter to the New England and mid-Atlantic state governors, requiring each of them to be prepared to raise militia and supplies in proportions as needed for a prospective impending major operation against New York City. He convened a grand council of war on June 6, during which he asked his general officers to prepare written position statements on how they believed Washington's army should coordinate military operations with the French.

On the same day, Samuel Huntington, president of the Continental Congress, wrote to Washington announcing that Congress felt it "expedient" to send Lee's corps, which Washington had detained, to South Carolina as soon as possible. Huntington did so equally at the behest of panic-stricken delegates and an impatient Lee, who was then in Philadelphia exerting pressure behind the scenes to secure him a combat assignment. Huntington added the qualification, though, that Washington should not comply if "his March to the Southward should counteract or embarrass such Plan of Operation as you may have concerted with Intention of employing that Corps otherwise." Washington freely made use of the qualification to keep Lee in place. Probably he was thinking of operations against New York, but the reprieve proved timely for another reason.[22]

IN NEW YORK, MAJOR GENERAL JAMES ROBERTSON, New Jersey royal governor William Franklin, and Knyphausen were fully cognizant of Washington's designs against their garrison. They were equally aware, by virtue of regular intelligence reports coming in from New Jersey via deserters and spies, of the severely weakened state of Washington's army. Conditions in New Jersey were indeed poor, not just for soldiers but for civilians. Just five years removed from their prerevolutionary positions in the royal government, the Loyalist leaders ate up reports of declining economic conditions in the former colonies and the impact this was having on civilian morale. Loyalties were never fixed on borderland states like New Jersey. Oppressed by the aftereffects of years of military campaigns over their lands, a brutal winter, and the collapse of the Continental currency, New Jersey civilians cooperated if not collaborated with the British, apparently in greater numbers than ever before. Although small numbers of militia had turned out quickly to fend off the raid on Newark, there was every reason to believe that in a major emergency the militia might fail to turn out in significant numbers.

The physically imposing and charismatic Franklin nurtured a deep grudge against the Americans for imprisoning him in Connecticut in 1777 while his wife died in New York City (he was exchanged, too late, the following year). He also felt certain that an enlightened British policy toward American Loyalists would uncover a deep well of fealty to the royal cause throughout the mid-Atlantic states. In this he found allies in Royal chief justice William Smith, former royal governor and now Major General William Tryon, and former barrack master Major General Robertson. All four felt that opportunities beckoned and that Clinton had been far too cautious in exploiting them.[23]

By the beginning of June their impatience had reached a tipping point. Correspondent after correspondent wrote to Smith and Franklin claiming that New Jersey was ripe for the picking. Clumps of deserters were coming in, escorted by Loyalists certain that Washington's army was falling apart. A little push, they insisted, would bring the whole rotten structure crashing down. Beckwith, then in secret correspondence with Major General Benedict Arnold, proved decisive. With Clinton victorious but still at sea, Beckwith concurred that a stroke could at worst do no real harm and just might change the course of the war. He and Tryon conferred with Knyphausen and got him to agree by June 5 on "an Experiment on the Temper of the Country and the Rebel Army."[24]

Knyphausen later summarized the arguments that had convinced him to endorse the "experiment." Washington, the Loyalist leaders claimed, had no more than 3,500 to 4,000 men at his disposal, below the threshold set by Beckwith. Those remaining behind after the detachment to Albany—about which Knyphausen had been informed—were "universally discontented" and tempted by the "general spirit of desertion." As for the militia, "tired of convulsions which they found pregnant with distress to themselves and families," they "were disposed to remain peaceably at home." "The moment," it seemed, "was too favourable to be lost."[25]

Still, "experiment" was the operative word. The post at Morristown was well chosen and practically impossible to take by surprise. It was about twenty miles from Elizabethtown Point, realistically the best landing and launching place. Even with a nighttime landing, daylight would certainly arise before the attackers were within striking distance of the main camp. And even if Maxwell's command broke and fled—a far-fetched proposition under the best of circumstances—the pass at Hobart Gap behind Springfield, about halfway to Morristown, could be held by any competent and determined adversary. (This happened, in fact, in December 1776, when a rebel command held the gap against a strong British reconnaissance in force.) A raid by a small force—as attempted in the abortive move to kidnap Washington in February—was one thing, a movement by a force of several thousand men another. Resistance of any significance raised the possibility of militia cutting off Knyphausen's lines of communication, supply, and retreat, meaning he would have to execute a swift withdrawal in case the enemy was able to hold him up. Still, if resistance proved too stout, a quick retreat should not be too challenging.

Knyphausen designated a strike force of about six thousand men, arranged in three attack and two reserve divisions under Brigadier General Thomas Stirling, Major General Edward Mathew, Major General William Tryon, General Carl Wilhelm von Hachenberg, and General Friedrich Wilhelm von Lossberg. Stirling's division included the British 37th and 38th Regiments of Foot, the German Leib and Landgraf Regiments, and two six-pounder cannon. Mathew's division consisted of the 22nd and 57th Regiments of Foot, a company of the 17th Regiment of Foot, the 1st and 4th Battalions of the Loyalist New Jersey Volunteers, a couple of three-pounder cannon, and a small cavalry detachment. The third division, under Tryon but accompanied by Knyphausen, was made up of the Jäger Corps (reduced at this time to a mere three hundred men because of detachments), the British Guards, and the 43rd Regiment of Foot. Hachenberg's reserve 4th Division included the Anspach and Bose regiments plus artillery, and Lossberg's reserve 5th Division included the Donop Regiment and the British 17th Dragoons (brought over hurriedly from Long Island) with artillery and baggage. The Bünau garrison regiment was designated as a baggage guard.[26]

Knyphausen intended for Stirling's division in flat-bottomed boats, and Tryon's division plus the reserve divisions, artillery, horses, and baggage on schooners and some other small ships, to sail from New York on the morning and afternoon of June 6 and land around midnight near Elizabethtown Point. They would then send the flat-bottomed boats across to Staten Island to fetch Mathew's division, while Tryon's division pushed ahead to seize Elizabethtown. Once united with Stirling and Mathew, the combined force of three attack divisions would push aggressively down the Galloping Hill Road seven miles to Springfield. If the going seemed easy at that point and a fast strike succeeded in capturing Hobart Gap a few miles farther up in the Short Hills, Knyphausen could unleash his combined force to march the remaining eleven, relatively easy miles to Morristown. At that point, he hoped to "have obliged General Washington to have quitted his camp at Morris Town, in which event he must have left a great part of his artillery and stores behind him for want of horses to carry them off or to have risked an action with a very inferior force."[27]

The plan was quite simple, amounting in military terms to little more than a probe, or reconnaissance in force. Still, the logistical preparations were considerable, as would be the expenditure of supplies and wear and tear on men and horses. Although the risks of major loss were slight, if the scheme failed, Knyphausen would have seriously degraded the forces under his command and so hindered his army's ability to carry out further operations in the near future. Knyphausen nevertheless judged it worth the risk. The main questions now were, could he take the enemy by surprise, and would the rebels fight? The answers would go a long way toward revealing the relative strengths of the pro- and anti-revolutionary forces at this point in the war—whose fortunes were on the rise, and whose were in decline. Both Washington and Knyphausen would be astonished by the truth.

The Battle of Connecticut Farms, June 7, 1780

UNITY OF COMMAND IS ONE OF THE prerequisites of a successful military campaign. The British army's deficiency in this regard became readily apparent as Knyphausen's troops prepared for action on the afternoon of June 6. Somewhere in the midst of the hurly-burly, Clinton's aide-de-camp, Major William Crosbie, showed up at Knyphausen's command post on Governor's Island. He would have arrived up to two weeks sooner, except that the captain of his transport frigate had held off from New York for several days for fear the British vessels he saw cruising offshore were actually French.

Crosbie carried a letter providing some details on the fall of Charleston, but also verbal instructions from Clinton to inform Knyphausen of his plans for further offensive operations in New Jersey once he had returned from the South at some uncertain future date. Not knowing anything of what would happen at New

York in the weeks following his dispatch of Crosbie, however, Clinton sensibly gave him discretion on whether to share any of this plan with the German general. If the French already were operating around New York, the plan would become moot and should be discarded.

Whether Crosbie and Knyphausen met at this time is unclear, and frankly unlikely. Thomas Fleming, author of the only modern book previously written on this subject, concocts a scenario of "The Anguished Aide-de-Camp," supposedly taking place among the harried generals on Governor's Island. According to Fleming, Crosbie agonized over his instructions to reveal only "hints" of Clinton's intentions. Baffled and annoyed, Knyphausen brushed those hints aside in his eagerness to carry out his own plans. Subsequent reports by Knyphausen and his adjutant, Major Carl Leopold von Baurmeister, however, indicate that the expeditionary force had already embarked and that Crosbie did not catch up to Knyphausen until he had already reached Connecticut Farms. Whether because of this, or because it was too late to cancel the attack, or Knyphausen and his officers preferred not to await the arrival of a commander whose aggressiveness they doubted, or Crosbie shared none or only a little of Clinton's plans for a future attack—the current expedition went forward, much to Clinton's future frustration. The whole affair reflects the difficulties of coordinating over significant distances of space and time and, to a somewhat lesser degree, indicates that Clinton and Knyphausen lacked the commonality of understanding that underpins the best command teams.[1]

Unfortunately for Knyphausen, his plans went awry almost immediately. Tryon's intended vanguard division embarked at New York at about 11:00 AM, followed by Stirling's division at about 3:00 PM. A "contrary wind" hindered their forward progress, however. Although the flat-bottomed boats carrying Stirling's division continued on to DeHart's Point near Elizabethtown Point on Newark Bay, where they debarked just before midnight, the ships carrying Tryon's division, and the others carrying the reserves, artillery, and baggage, could not follow them as planned and had to unload at Decker's Ferry on Staten Island. From there they marched to Garrett Post House opposite Elizabethtown Point.

Getting across to New Jersey from there was far from easy. Because the tide was low, leaving water channels snaking across the mudflats on shore, the flatboats Stirling dispatched to Staten Island were unable to rendezvous with the troops waiting onshore. British engineers hurriedly constructed small bridges to traverse those channels, but the process took a few hours. Since Mathew's division was already prepared for the crossing, it boarded the boats first just as the sun began coming up. Tryon's division, less organized after having had to debark and march to Garret's Post House, followed in Mathew's train. Instead of leading the push into New Jersey with the Jäger Corps and British Guards, Knyphausen would have to take up the rear with the remainder of Tryon's troops.[2]

This unanticipated change was to cost Stirling his life. Informed that he was to take the van, the general advanced at the head of his force toward Elizabethtown in the early minutes of June 7. A long-time soldier, Stirling had served in North America during the French and Indian War and was no fan of the land or its people. "I am heartily tired of this country as is every officer in it," he wrote home in 1760 from Montreal while serving as a lieutenant with the Black Watch. "[L]ong may Peace reign here, for sure god never intended any war should be carried on by any other besides the natives." Now he was approaching a spot where the roads from DeHart's Point and Elizabethtown Point met about a mile outside Elizabethtown. Suddenly a small band of Continentals opened fire, and a musket ball shattered Stirling's thigh. He had one more reason to hate America.[3]

On the opposite side, Colonel Elias Dayton proved quickly that he was the right man to keep point. Born in Elizabethtown, where he operated a store and of which he would later serve as mayor, Dayton was a veteran soldier who had also seen action in the French and Indian War. He knew all of the local people and every inch of the ground thereabouts. Informed of Stirling's landing as soon as it occurred and possibly earlier, he had dispatched Ensign Moses Ogden of Spencer's Additional Continental Regiment to take post at the crossroads with twelve men while Dayton formed the bulk of his two regiments on Jelf's Hill behind a stone bridge in Elizabethtown. He also sent word to alert Maxwell at West Farms.

Ogden's detachment assembled in a pasture owned by his avidly patriotic family west of the crossroads, from where they opened fire on the approaching British column, wounding Stirling in the thigh. After the discharge, and probably hearing the British general cry out in pain, Ogden and his men fled back to Jelf's Hill. Colonel Dayton received them and had his son Captain Jonathan Dayton write to Washington, "the enemy landed this night at 12 oClock, from the best intelligence four or five thousand men & Twelve field pieces, & it is his conjecture they intend to penetrate into the country."[4]

Meanwhile, shocked by this unexpected encounter and the loss of its commander, the British column lurched to a halt. Command fell to Colonel Friedrich Wilhelm von Wurmb, commanding the Prince's Own Leib Regiment, "garde du corps." This regiment, composed of men handpicked for their stature and strength, was of a higher grade than most, and so was Colonel Wurmb. He was "clear headed and cool," remarked a British officer. "He serves with zeal, and is attentive only to establish his Character as a Soldier and an honest man." Still, distracted by the need to care for Stirling and possibly not entirely sure of his responsibilities, Wurmb elected to halt for reorganization and further instructions.[5]

While Wurmb waited, Washington received Captain Dayton's letter at 4:00 AM. Already, Knyphausen had lost the element of surprise. The commander in chief responded to the intelligence decisively, alerting his officers to hold their troops "in readiness to march at a moment's warning," and to issue each man forty rounds of ammunition and provisions for two days. Three hours later, evidently after poring over maps and conferring with his general officers, Washington ordered the bulk of his six brigades to march for Chatham on the road to Springfield. He would lead them in person. The 2nd Connecticut and 1st Connecticut Brigades, numbering just over 1,000 men, took the lead. They were followed by Brigadier General John Stark's and Brigadier General Edward Hand's brigades, totaling about 1,400 troops, and then the 2nd and 1st Pennsylvania Brigades, with about 1,800 men. At 4,200 men, it was a paltry force; Maxwell had about 800 more.[6]

The only way to augment these numbers was to call out the militia, and Washington wrote to General Alexander to that purpose before beginning his own march. Further intelligence, probably verbal, having told Washington that the enemy was on the move from Elizabethtown to Springfield, the commander in chief ordered Alexander "to give the alarm as extensively as you can in your quarter and to remain to form them as they collect and march them towards the enemy." At 8:30 AM, not having personally left headquarters yet, Washington wrote to Major Jeremiah Talbot, commanding a small detachment of perhaps a few dozen men at Paramus, New Jersey. He told Talbot to share the alarm with all militia detachments in the vicinity and then to make haste for Chatham with his own detachment while sending scouts and couriers to keep watch for the enemy. At around the same time, Washington had his aide-de-camp, Lieutenant Colonel Alexander Hamilton, write to Major General Steuben, then out on his rounds, informing him of the events and asking him to meet the main army at Chatham.

In his letter to Alexander, Washington confessed his continuing uncertainty over whether the enemy "may aim at our camp or . . . only intend to proceed as far as the mountains and file off to the left making a sweep of all the forage Cattle &c. in their way." Whatever their intention, the obvious move was to place his main force at Chatham to protect Hobart Gap, allowing the Continental army to either make a stand or advance on Springfield with a secure line of supply and retreat. Had matters reached that pass and an extended contest with Knyphausen taken place, Washington would have been able to call upon two thousand militiamen from Middlesex, Somerset, Essex, and Morris Counties who came out over the next few days in response to an urgent call from Alexander, who meanwhile gathered every active militiaman he could find in the vicinity and hurried off to Springfield.[7]

As Washington prepared his troops for the move to Chatham, at the first glimmerings of dawn Wurmb resumed his march, leaving the ill-starred crossroads and passing through Elizabethtown toward its northwest edge. Leaving the central town, with its burnt-out buildings serving as testimony to the destructive January raid, they crossed the stone bridge over the Elizabeth River, passed Jelf's Hill, and then headed north-northwest on the Galloping Hill Road toward Springfield.

Wurmb's advance was unopposed. During the night, Dayton had abandoned Jelf's Hill and pulled back to Connecticut Farms. This meant abandoning not only Elizabethtown but Governor William Livingston's mansion about two miles northwest of town, Liberty Hall. Livingston had completed the home only several years before the war swept over New Jersey, although he could not afford to live there for long periods during the hostilities. He was a marked man, and Loyalists more than once contemplated capturing him. Thus the governor spent considerable time in the state's interior out of harm's way. But, trusting to British chivalry and the accepted rules of war that supposedly protected unoffending civilians, Livingston allowed his daughters to remain at Liberty Hall. Wurmb arrived there with his advance guard at about 6:00 AM. The romantic local tales of what may or may not have transpired as the gallant German colonel met the governor's delightful daughter Susan need not concern us here; suffice to say that Wurmb appears to have placed a guard on the house for the safety of its inhabitants before moving on.[8] Liberty Hall survives today, apparently in part thanks to the colonel.

Long before the sun rose, other glimmerings had appeared atop eminences in the Watchung Mountains and elsewhere. These were signal beacons—sometimes signal cannon boomed too—intended to rouse the New Jersey militia and warn civilians to the approaching enemy. As Wurmb's force continued past Liberty Hall, it took scattering fire from Continental detachments and militia posted in an orchard behind the governor's mansion, and on rising ground just beyond the west branch of the Elizabeth River, about a quarter mile southeast of Connecticut Farms meeting house. The militia also wrecked a couple of small bridges crossing boggy creeks, further slowing the British and German soldiers. Wurmb easily dispersed the militia skirmishers, but they continued to increase in numbers.[9]

WORD SPREAD QUICKLY to local civilians that trouble was imminent. Long before the militia and the American regulars began taking potshots at Wurmb's men, residents of Connecticut Farms read the portents. Something clearly was in the offing, and they prepared for the worst. Their village was a small one, a straggling settlement of a meeting house and a few dozen small wooden houses lining a two-mile stretch of the Galloping Hill Road. It was only four miles west of Elizabethtown, one of New Jersey's original municipalities; and the hamlet was actually a part of Elizabethtown and fell under the jurisdiction of the larger town's laws and courts. (It became independent as today's Union only in 1808.)

First settled in 1667, the area originally was known as Wade's Farms; but it quickly became Connecticut Farms, taking its name from the New England origins of many of the arriving families. It was a pleasant locale with gently undulating, rich soil, "well watered by branches of the Rahway and Elizabeth Rivers." Residents were mostly middling farmers, and holdings of less than 20 acres to over 150 supported crops of grain, fruit orchards, cattle and other livestock, and ample stands of timber. Riding through the region on one occasion, an impressed Washington supposedly called Connecticut Farms "the Garden of New Jersey."[10] If Washington actually said it, his impression was accurate.

The "Garden," however, was directly on the route Knyphausen had to take if he was to drive through to Hobart Gap and beyond. Once the British had landed at Elizabethtown and got organized, it would not take them long to reach their village. Faced with this unpleasant reality, civilians followed what by this time was a standard drill for towns in eastern New Jersey: upon hearing a signal gun (or receiving some other warning), they hid any valuables they couldn't carry off, drove livestock into the woods, collected their families, and scattered. For residents of Connecticut Farms, that generally meant moving west to the Short Hills, or even farther to the Watchung Mountains.

The hasty evacuation was effective; when Knyphausen arrived at the village, he found it well-nigh empty. Only a few families had remained. This left most homes and other structures, not to mention crops, which by June were well along, prey to any depredations the enemy might inflict. But as we will see, it kept civilian casualties to a minimum. What Connecticut Farms and other settlements along the Galloping Hill Road had yet to learn, however, was that they faced more than the typical small-scale raid.

THE DELAYING ACTIONS in front of Connecticut Farms took place at Maxwell's behest. Stationed with the 1st and 2nd New Jersey Regiments in his camp at West Farms, he received news of the enemy incursion just before midnight, and threw his force in motion toward Elizabethtown. At the same time, he dispatched his aide-de-camp, Major Aaron Ogden (uncle to Moses) ahead on horseback to make contact with Dayton. Ogden met Dayton on Jelf's Hill, while Maxwell marched his force four miles to Liberty Hall. Informed of the invaders' superior strength, Maxwell concluded that Elizabethtown was too far out of range of effective support and thus an "improper place" to make a stand. He ordered the New Jersey Brigade to pull back again to Connecticut Farms. As Dayton withdrew, he sent small detachments of Continentals to coordinate with local militia in screening the enemy and delaying it where possible.[11]

Connecticut Farms was a straggling settlement of a meeting house and a few dozen small wooden houses lining a two-mile

stretch of the Galloping Hill Road. Presumably on Maxwell's orders, elements of Dayton's and Spencer's regiments occupied a
defile along the settlement's eastern edge, "near the farm meeting house, where they were joined and assisted in the defense by
some small bodies of militia." Maxwell prudently retained the remainder of his force some distance farther back, protecting "the
roads leading to the right and left" around Connecticut Farms
and toward Springfield lest Wurmb attempt to cut him off. Since
Maxwell's whole purpose was to delay the enemy while waiting
for Washington to arrive and the militia turn out in strength, this
arrangement made perfect sense.[12]

Whether Maxwell or Dayton chose the post at the defile is uncertain. But the position was strong, and so were the "small parties" of officers and men who defended it. Dayton was in overall
command there. His second, since Colonel Oliver Spencer apparently was not present (perhaps because of court-martial duties), was Lieutenant Colonel William Stephens Smith of
Spencer's regiment. A New Yorker who had graduated from the
College of New Jersey and would later marry John Adams's
daughter and serve in Congress, Smith was a gossip and trouble-
maker. He was also a confident officer, and that was just as well,
for in the strange circumstances of June 1780, he at one time or
another found himself in command of three out of four regiments in the New Jersey Brigade, and at least once, as now, in
command of two at the same time. On the morning of June 7,
Colonel Matthias Ogden, commanding the 1st Regiment but re-
cuperating from an illness, asked Smith to take command of a
temporarily merged command of the 1st and Spencer's regiments
once he returned from the defile.[13]

Dayton and Smith worked well together and were exceptionally aggressive despite their small (now indeterminate) numbers.
"Our parties of Continental troops and militia at the defile performed wonders," Maxwell later informed Governor Livingston,
and they managed to hold up Wurmb's advance guard for "near
three hours" (although that was probably more an impression
than reality). As always in affairs of this sort, the details remain

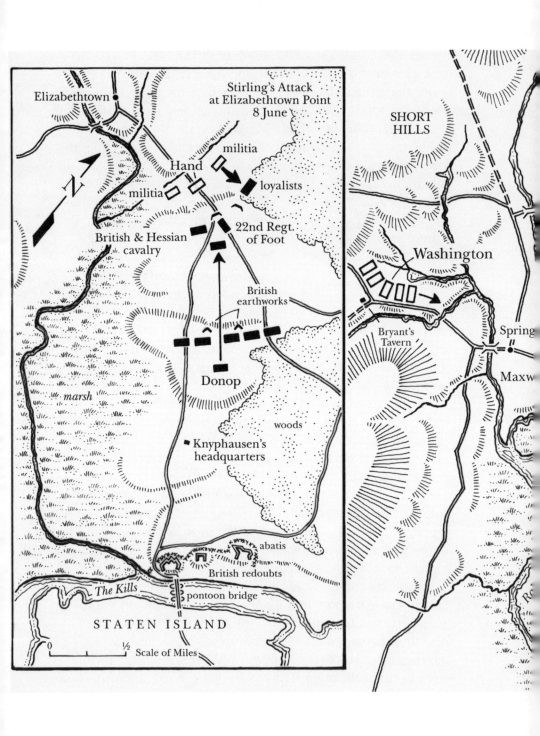

Elizabethtown

Stirling's Attack
at Elizabethtown Point
8 June

SHORT
HILLS

militia

Hand

militia

loyalists

22nd Regt.
of Foot

British & Hessian
cavalry

Washington

British
earthworks

Donop

Bryant's
Tavern

Spring

Maxw

woods

Knyphausen's
headquarters

marsh

abatis

British redoubts

The Kills

pontoon bridge

STATEN ISLAND

0   ½   Scale of Miles

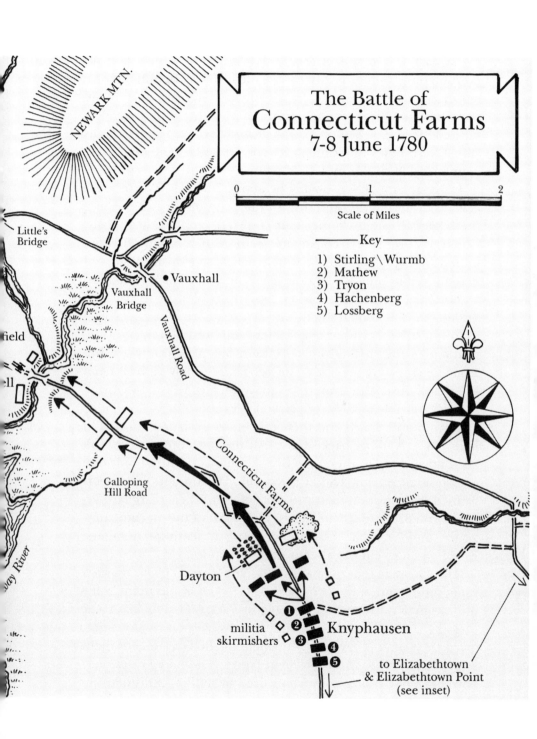

The Battle of
Connecticut Farms
7-8 June 1780

0   1   2

Scale of Miles

——— Key ———

1) Stirling \ Wurmb
2) Mathew
3) Tryon
4) Hachenberg
5) Lossberg

NEWARK MTN.

Little's
Bridge

Vauxhall

Vauxhall
Bridge

Vauxhall Road

field

ll

Galloping
Hill Road

Connecticut Farms

Dayton

ay River

militia
skirmishers

Knyphausen

to Elizabethtown
& Elizabethtown Point
(see inset)

confused, but it would appear that Wurmb probed the American position only cautiously. After some inconclusive fighting, the attackers appeared disorganized. Dayton, perhaps recognizing the need to make his force seem more powerful than it really was, pushed the enemy back at least once and perhaps twice, as far as "the Tavern that was Jacamiah Smiths," despite some ineffective counterfire from Wurmb's field pieces.[14]

In time, though—probably by about 7:30 AM—Wurmb succeeded in prying the Americans out of the defile and pushing them back through Connecticut Farms. Soon afterward, Major General Mathew arrived on the scene with the 2nd Division, joined by the Jäger Corps, which had raced up in a "forced march" to join him. Placing the jäger in the lead as Knyphausen had originally intended, Mathew moved past Wurmb to clear the settlement. The remainder of Knyphausen's 3rd Division arrived at Connecticut Farms at 8:00 AM and followed behind. In Connecticut Farms, small groups of Americans paused to open fire from hedges and houses. "The rebels generally retired from house to house, and from wood to wood, and resisted their foe in every possible way," Knyphausen later reported.[15]

Dayton and Smith and their officers kept their men well in hand, never pulling back so fast that the detachments couldn't keep up and rejoin them; the British Guards captured only one or two men. As they had at the defile, Dayton and Smith performed their mission nearly to perfection in their rearguard action through Connecticut Farms. With most of the morning now gone and militia assembling in increasing numbers, Knyphausen's plan was already on life support.

The German general may in fact have already given up on a rapid movement, if the behavior of his troops at this point is any indication. For rather than keeping his men on a tight leash and pressing them forward—probably impossible now in any event, given their level of fatigue—Knyphausen allowed some of them to get out of hand in Connecticut Farms. The initial cause may have been one of many: potshots fired by militia (indistinguishable from civilians) from buildings and yards, anger at Stirling's wounding as yet another example of how the Americans targeted officers, or disappointment. Whatever the incitement, German and British troops began breaking into homes, causing damage, and carrying out some looting. Their conduct may or may not have been defensible according to the rules of war as then understood—it depends on whether Americans fired on them from inside civilian homes, which is now impossible to confirm or deny. From the military standpoint, however, such conduct while fighting still raged was redolent of disorder, and so indefensible; and it also served to infuriate the enemy.[16]

The grisly fate of Hannah Caldwell gave these atrocities a human face, and a martyr whom the Americans in New Jersey could rally around. Her husband's efforts on behalf of the rebels were well known, certainly to the Loyalists with the invading force, and some among them appear to have sought him out. They had reason enough to hate him. In January 1780, raiders from New York (likely vengeful Tories) had burned his church in Elizabethtown, after which the Rev. Caldwell moved his family to Connecticut Farms. The setback in Elizabethtown did nothing to cow him. The furious pastor did everything in his power to rally Jerseymen to the rebel cause, and he was notorious for his fiery invective against the British. Known as the "Fighting Parson," Caldwell served in the field as a chaplain in Maxwell's New Jersey Brigade. He was with the army in Morristown when Knyphausen's command fought its way through Connecticut Farms. Caldwell's family, however, was one of the few still in town.

The result was tragedy. "Following the absurd principles of too many of our incautious countrymen," according to a critical account, he left his wife, children, and maid at home in hopes that an enemy who had been gallant enough to leave the Livingston family unharmed would also leave them alone. But he had no such luck. According to rebel accounts, a German soldier or a British redcoat deliberately shot Hannah Caldwell to death through a window as she huddled with her maid and children. The soldiers then torched her house. The rest of her family escaped harm, however, and her body was buried outside instead of being left to go up in flames with her home. The truth of what happened is now impossible to ascertain, but in some ways it hardly mattered: Hannah Caldwell's fate made for useful propaganda.[17] The American press, and the widowed James Caldwell himself in a long and angry pamphlet, excoriated British perfidy and blamed Hannah's death on orders from the highest reaches of the enemy command. The affair was reminiscent of the Jane McCrea incident that so embarrassed John Burgoyne in 1777. Fervent British denials of a deliberate killing notwithstanding, Americans believed the worst.[18]

While the Hannah Caldwell tragedy unfolded, the fighting around the village continued. Maxwell later reported to Governor Livingston that he had formed up his entire brigade in preparation for a possible all-out counterattack against the enemy column. Apparently after consultation with his officers, however, "it was thought imprudent, as the ground was not advantageous and the enemy very numerous." Instead, he pulled back his command slowly toward Springfield, climbing the heights just east of a bridge over the Rahway River. Along the way he kept pressure on Knyphausen with skirmishing parties. This continued until, Maxwell claimed, Knyphausen's advance reached David Meeker's House on the western outskirts of Connecticut Farms and halted there, probably around 9:00 or 9:30 AM.

Knyphausen deployed his forces into two lines, with the Jäger Corps and the British Guards in front. Here the king's forces remained for almost two hours, their leader later justifying the delay by claiming he was waiting for the slow-moving reserves, artillery, and baggage to join him. Sensing an opportunity, Maxwell ordered an immediate attack with "the whole Brigade with the militia . . . on their right, left & front." His troops attacked at 11:00 AM and advanced, he later reported in a brief and unilluminating account, "with the greatest rapidity," pushing the enemy advance guard back to Knyphausen's main body some distance behind.

Smith, by contrast, left a more complex description of these events that suggests more hurry and a certain degree of confusion on the Americans' part. After withdrawing with Dayton from Con-

THE BATTLE OF CONNECTICUT FARMS, JUNE 7, 1780

necticut Farms, Smith recalled, he met with Maxwell at the head of the remainder of the brigade somewhere near the bridge. Smith (Dayton disappears from his account at this point—perhaps his tired regiment was ordered back to the bridge) there took charge of his mixed command, including Spencer's regiment and Ogden's 1st New Jersey Regiment.

Maxwell and Smith walked down to the foot of the slope, and the general ordered the lieutenant colonel to detach three platoons about one hundred yards to the right of Galloping Hill Road. A few minutes later, he told Smith to send another three platoons about the same distance to the left. This, with unspecified "detachments previously made," left Smith and his remaining command in front of the 2nd New Jersey Regiment under Colonel Israel Shreve, whom Smith claimed preferred to lead his regiment from the rear.

Judging that he should remain in the center of his divided command so he could retain contact with and if necessary support either wing, Smith continued forward until Meeker's house came into view and the flanking parties began to exchange fire with Knyphausen's troops. According to Smith, the American attack ran smack dab into the Jäger Corps, which was "ready to receive them" but apparently fell back under pressure some distance behind the Meeker house.

The jäger were surprised and impressed by the Americans' audacity. "The enemy continued to fire and pressed forward several times with the bayonet and new reinforcements," reported the corps journal. "As often as he was beaten back, so often he returned with a fresh attack." British Guards light infantry then moved forward and joined the Germans in forcing the Americans back. George Mathew, who was a lieutenant in the British Guards and nephew of the general, exulted, "The rebels no sooner saw us than they ran off as hard as they could. They ran much faster than we. They are of a thin, long-legged make; most of them without shoes and stockings and without coats, and sometimes they throw away their arms when closely pursued."[19]

Nervously, Maxwell asked Smith "if I did not think it best to detach a platoon to Meeker's house, which he said was sufficient to support the road and prevent the enemy from pressing through and separating the detachments mentioned." Smith demurred, arguing that a mere platoon at the house would be annihilated and that even the remainder of his mixed regiment "was not equal to the task." As they conferred, Knyphausen's troops appeared directly ahead down the road, engaging the Americans "in a tolerable fire." Seeing this, Maxwell "turn'd his horse and told me to do what I thought proper and left me."

The fighting now centered on the lieutenant colonel and his command. Despite his earlier suggestion that his regiment would not suffice to hold the house, Smith, for whatever reason, now ordered his men to advance at an all-out run with the enemy pressing forward at equal speed from the opposite side—a strange decision on all accounts, also given the enemy's superiority with the bayonet, although it did suggest that Smith was commanding in Maxwell and Shreve's absence. In any event, according to Smith, the Americans reached Meeker's House first, with the enemy still thirty to forty yards away. There then commenced "a smart skirmish," but as Smith had predicted, his force was unable to hold. Pressed in front and then outflanked on the left, Smith ordered his men to retreat as quickly as they had advanced.

Maxwell wrote little about this encounter except that it was "the closest action I have seen this war," and ended with his brigade being pushed back over the bridge. Smith's account continued in its imputations of cowardice against Maxwell and especially Shreve. The former, evidently, simply disappeared, while Shreve abandoned his command. In his own withdrawal, Smith took up the 2nd Regiment—evidently unengaged up to this point—and pulled all three regiments back to the top of the hill east of the bridge. There he found Shreve "mixing with a group of spectators who stood a tip-toe ready to move to the next commanding ground upon the approach of danger." From there, said Smith, the enemy "continuing a rapid advance upon our left thro' the wood forced us from the hill and pressed us hard over the bridge."[20]

Knyphausen reported that the Americans withdrew behind the bridge, "pelted by the guns," but he made no serious attempt to seize it. Maxwell had smartly prepared defensive positions there, possibly even—if Smith's account is to be believed—while the action was taking place at Meeker's House. In any event, the Americans took post in good order at the bridge and some distance along the river on either side, backed up by one small cannon, possibly two, brought up by the militia. They put this cannon to use in driving back a couple of enemy probes toward the bridge, after which Knyphausen's forces pulled back. A small-scale artillery duel then commenced between a couple of guns on either side.[21]

Knyphausen later claimed to have realized at this point that he had no chance of seizing Hobart Gap before nightfall. Still, he thought it realistic to take Springfield, "force the pass" into the Short Hills beyond, and "advance a few miles in order to take up a more advantageous position than the present one"—provided his two reserve divisions with artillery and baggage came up in time. And so he waited—and waited. At 2:00 PM, Major General Robertson, though accompanying the expedition without official command, arrived with the Bünau Garrison Regiment, which he had "thought proper"—to Knyphausen's evident annoyance—to bring with him from its guard posting at Elizabethtown Point. Hachenberg's division appeared two hours later, but Lossberg still lagged behind near Liberty Hall. While he waited, Knyphausen ordered the construction of a temporary defensive breastwork along Galloping Hill Road west of Connecticut Farms, which his troops now took to plundering with a will.[22]

This extended delay, with the construction of a breastwork and the looting of Connecticut Farms, fails to jibe with Knyphausen's avowed intention of driving hard and fast toward Hobart Gap. His after-action report blames early morning adverse winds, the slowness of Hachenberg and Lossberg, and intensifying opposition from American militia for his inability to move more quickly.

Crosbie's arrival at Connecticut Farms during the late afternoon with news of Clinton's impending arrival from Charleston provided an opportunity to formally cancel the attack. Knyphausen conferred with his generals and decided to withdraw that evening, while sending orders to Lossberg to halt and await the main body at Liberty Hall. By this point, however, Knyphausen had already remained supine for several hours—at least since midmorning, except for repelling Maxwell's attack at 11:00 AM. Why, unless he had already essentially discarded his plans after occupying Connecticut Farms?[23]

Perhaps anticipating Washington's imminent arrival, meanwhile, Maxwell sent some of his light troops back across the Rahway to skirmish with, and keep an eye on, the enemy. The commander in chief was by that point, in midafternoon, already in the Short Hills just behind Springfield, deploying his troops for possible defensive action. Washington assembled a detachment of his personal guards, plus some regular Continentals under the command of Major Caleb Gibbs and Lieutenant William Colfax, and sent them forward to support Maxwell. The impetuous Gibbs—no doubt encouraged by Washington to make a show of force if possible—marched his detachment right across the river as the sun was setting and, without trying to find Maxwell (whom he only informed the following day), gave "the Hessian Lads a Charge . . . & drove them merrily." As the Germans—in reality, just pickets—fled, Gibbs ordered his troops to fire an astonishing eight utterly useless volleys at their figures disappearing in the distance. The Jäger Corps then appeared and drove the Americans "back a great distance" (a comeuppance not mentioned by Gibbs in his report). This piece of playacting cost a handful of casualties on both sides.[24]

In the Short Hills, Washington deployed his Pennsylvania division on the right under Major General Nathanael Greene and the Connecticut division on the left under Major General Lafayette. Major General Steuben, who appeared to awe young militiaman Ashbel Green like "a perfect personification of Mars," commanded Brigadier General John Stark's and Brigadier General Edward Hand's brigades in support, detaching two regiments to guard the road north to Newark Mountain. Although officially designated an "advance corps," Maxwell's tired New Jersey Brigade bedded down for the night on a ridge about three quarters of a mile west of Springfield. The men were to "lie on their Arms and the Officers with their respective regiments and platoons [so] that in Case of an alarm every officer and man may be immediately at his Post."[25]

After sunset, Washington assembled his officers in council of war to decide what to do next. In the conference, he at least considered—backed by his cocky officers—the possibility of launching a night attack on Knyphausen. Allegedly this was to take place in the early morning hours, but no sources beyond Nathanael Greene's much later correspondence with William Gordon suggests any preparations for such an attack were put in motion (Ashbel Green, in fact, describes Washington's efforts to set a trap convincing Knyphausen to attack him). In any event, the weather put an end to this dubious proposition, as a heavy rain commenced after midnight. The militia, though, had kept the pressure on for most of the evening, harassing Knyphausen's troops in the breastwork and surrounding woods; and although they had been able to do nothing to check the horrors in Connecticut Farms, they induced the Germans to waste much of their ammunition.[26]

As Washington conferred with his officers, Knyphausen dropped the leash and gave his troops liberty to do as they pleased in Connecticut Farms—specifically ordering them, allegedly at the urging of Tryon, who had carried out similar conduct in Connecticut in 1779, to torch the place. They did so, leaving only two buildings standing. Tryon, along with many other Loyalist and British officers, was a "hard line" man who believed the only way to win the war was to wage it with fire and sword. From his perspective, the orders to burn the village were understandable if, as he no doubt believed, the Americans used civilian residences for cover during their withdrawal from Connecticut Farms. This would have justified their immolation according to most interpretations of the rules of eighteenth-century warfare. At least some of those houses, in any event, were the property of militiamen.[27] The village was not the first, nor would it be the last, to suffer accordingly.

With buildings still in flames or smoldering, at 9:00 PM orders came down to pack up and march back toward Elizabethtown, abandoning the ruins of Connecticut Farms and the impromptu breastwork.[28] "Nothing more awful that this retreat can be imagined," Lieutenant Mathew later wrote in his diary. When they began their retreat the night was so dark, thanks to lowering storm clouds, that units (including Mathew's picket) lost touch with each other. Then the skies opened. "The rain, with the terrible thunder and lightning, the darkness of the night, the houses at Connecticut Farms, which we had set fire to, the dead bodies which the lightning showed you now and then on the road, and the dread of an enemy completed this scene of horror." At times the storm became so intense that the column had to halt for lack of visibility. Knyphausen's horse, panicked by a blast of thunder, threw the general, who was fortunately unhurt.[29]

The weather kept the Americans hunkered down too, and it was not until daybreak that Gibbs sent a scout and two dragoons out to reconnoiter. They returned quickly, dragging along an enemy straggler who confessed that the invaders had left around midnight but claimed he did not know by what route. Gibbs fired off a letter to Maxwell with the news, then departed to try to find the enemy. Informed of Knyphausen's withdrawal, which cannot have come as a surprise, Washington remained cautious. Riding to the heights above Springfield on the east side of the Rahway, he issued orders for his three division commanders to supply six hundred men to form a three-battalion detachment under Brigadier General Hand, which would follow up the enemy when ready. The main body of his force, however, would remain in place.[30]

Washington then had Hamilton draft a letter to Alexander, informing him of the formation of Hand's detachment, which was "to be employed to day as actively as the situation of the enemy will permit in conjunction with the Militia." By virtue of his rank, Alexander would assume command over the whole. Washington warned him, though, to keep his force in the woods as the means best suited to harass Knyphausen, while ensuring security against any enemy cavalry. Once Alexander had his militia "put into some form" and tried to ascertain their numbers, he was to "permit them to act in their own way—having places of rendezvous to assemble occasionally—& receive orders." This work done, Washington sent Hamilton off to assess the situation and act as the commander in chief's representative at the front.[31]

Alexander dutifully echoed the same note of caution in his own orders to the militia commanders. Although they were to "be as active as possible in annoying the Enemy this Day" with all the forces at their disposal, they were to remain "as much covered by Woods as the situation of the Country will admit," beware of enemy cavalry, and conserve ammunition. This spirit did not last long—no doubt in part because the burning of Connecticut Farms, in conjunction with earlier raids, brought the Americans to such a pitch of rage that they could not be held back. "The distress occasioned by their devastations is too shocking to reflect on," wrote one Continental officer who entered Connecticut Farms that morning and discovered a young woman who had been brutally raped. "[A]n American who could have beheld the scene and not swore vengeance against these savage enemies, ought to have a mark set on him as a curse to the human species."[32]

Hand's detachment passed through the remnants of the village that morning, and Alexander met it on the road to Elizabethtown. By that time, Alexander had reconnoitered Knyphausen's position at Elizabethtown Point and decided it was vulnerable— or at least its outposts were. Outside Elizabethtown, just under half a mile to the east, Knyphausen had stationed two forward detachments: elements of the 22nd Regiment of Foot on the left, manning a barricade at a fork on the road to the shore, with a small group of British and German cavalry roving about to their left; and Loyalist troops in a point of woods about five hundred feet to the right. Another half mile to the east stood Knyphausen's headquarters, screened by his German infantry. From Elizabethtown the defensive perimeter did not look too formidable; and besides, Knyphausen appeared to be in great haste, having already sent his wagons, many of his horses, and part of his artillery over to Staten Island. No large forces of cavalry appeared to be present.[33]

Writing long after the event, Ashbel Green left an account of what happened next. Alexander, surmising that most of Knyphausen's infantry had departed to Staten Island as well, told Hand to take his force and two brigades of militia and "go down and bring up those fellows at the Point." Hand, an Irish-born doctor who had acquired a reputation for aggressiveness and even bloodthirstiness in battle under Washington and along the frontier, "was nothing loth to attempt the execution of this order." Hand assembled his troops at Elizabethtown and arranged them in three columns, Hand commanding the Continentals in the center with militia brigades on either side. They were to march separately and attack the enemy concentrically and simultaneously at about 8:00 AM. Maneuver of this sort was a lot to ask Continentals, let alone militia, as Washington had learned before to his sorrow. And Hand, a stranger to these parts, took little measure of the terrain.

Green made no further mention in his account of the right-hand militia column, which would make sense, since if Hand indeed sent it off to the right, it must have become bogged down in a salt marsh on either side of Elizabethtown Creek. The left-hand militia column, which Green accompanied, struggled to cross fences and ditches before entering a meadow immediately opposite the woods held by the Loyalists. The gist of the story seems to be that the Loyalists opened fire, and the militia prudently retired. In Green's telling, though, the militia walked into a veritable inferno of "cannon balls and grape shot which from right to left they poured forth, and which swept over us, as we were passing the meadow. . . . It was a special mercy that they overshot us, otherwise the carnage must have been horrible." This was, of course, a ludicrous overstatement, and no British artillery appears to have come into play in this episode.[34]

As for Hand with his Continentals, they captured a small picket guard—according to Green, the red-coated prisoners and their captors were then fired upon by trigger-happy militia—and pressed the barricade held by the 22nd Foot, inflicting some casualties. The British troops "retired under orders," from the barricade, whereupon Knyphausen sent up the Donop, Bose, and Anspach Regiments to beat back what one young German officer called "an astonishing number of rebels." Their appearance was sufficient to dictate an American retreat. Green recounted an elaborate ruse, by which Hand attempted to convince the enemy that his advance was only a feint by ordering his respective brigades to retire "not precipitately, but as if they were only executing a manœuvre;" so that they might draw Knyphausen's forces out of their entrenchments and so pounce upon them. More likely, Hand simply ordered, and his troops executed, an orderly withdrawal to Elizabethtown.[35]

Hamilton wrote to Washington, probably in the afternoon as skirmishing continued in the vicinity, that he judged Knyphausen still had about three thousand troops at the point, although he confirmed that much of horse, baggage, and artillery had already been sent back to Staten Island. Considering the possibilities—including that the whole thing was a trap designed to draw out the Americans—Hamilton surmised that Knyphausen did not judge it safe to attempt a withdrawal over Arthur Kill by boat with evidently strong and aggressive American forces to his immediate front. Alexander reported to Washington at five o'clock that the enemy remained too strong to attack and recommended halting the main force of the army two to three miles in the rear.[36]

Washington received these reports at the scorched remains of Connecticut Farms meeting house, where he had halted the head of his column. Writing back at sunset, he told Alexander he would keep his troops lying on their arms and ordered him to report instantly if it looked like the enemy was about to attempt an immediate evacuation by boat. In that case, he said, he would consider

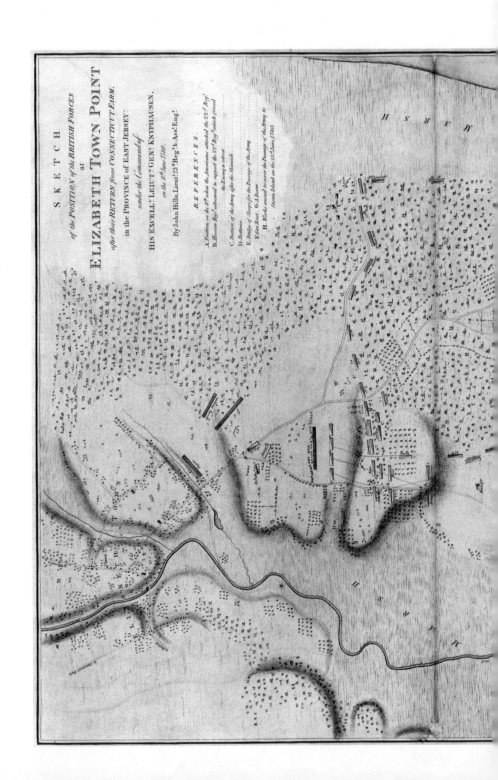

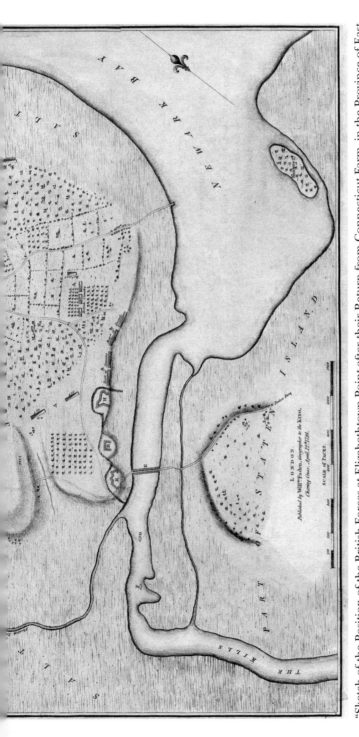

"Sketch of the Position of the British Forces at Elizabethtown Point after their Return from Connecticut Farm, in the Province of East Jersey: under the Command of His Excelly Leiutt Genl. Knyphausen, on the 8th June 1780," by John Hills. (*Library of Congress*)

a move against them. But he remained abundantly cautious. Alexander must make absolutely certain of the enemy's vulnerability before advising an attack, "as our moving otherwise might lead to very serious consequence." Moreover, Alexander was to employ not only "Centries & patroles" to guard against a sudden direct attack from Knyphausen but also "some Horsemen & trusty persons" to keep watch lest Knyphausen initiate another drive inland. In the meanwhile, Alexander was to pull back his own force well behind Elizabethtown for its security—a move Alexander heartily approved of and promptly carried out.[37]

With that, the Battle of Connecticut Farms came to an end. American casualties for June 7–8 were insignificant; Maxwell counted thirty-six lost from the forces under his command, and the militia probably incurred a dozen or two. As after every battle, American "eyewitnesses," including Maxwell, recounted stories—usually second or third hand—of heaps of enemy dead and wounded. The Americans also reported capturing thirty to forty enemy soldiers, probably mostly stragglers. Knyphausen reported 11 dead, 145 wounded, and 37 missing, with the heaviest casualties being incurred by the Jäger Corps (probably in the 11:00 AM American attack), the Leib Regiment (likely at the defile and in Connecticut Farms), and the 22nd Regiment of Foot (in the June 8 American attack).[38]

As the lopsided casualty figures would suggest, the expedition was for Knyphausen an unmitigated failure. Except for burning Connecticut Farms and further enraging the people of eastern New Jersey, his force had wasted men and resources and accomplished precisely nothing. The German general himself had demonstrated slipshod military management, failing to move or coordinate his divided forces effectively and not keeping them under firm control on the battlefield. Although the loss of Major General Stirling at the outset undoubtedly hurt, it does not excuse Knyphausen's lackadaisical conduct. He appears to have lost faith in the venture very quickly—as early as midmorning—and inevitably his officers and men followed his example.

On the American side, there were two outstanding positives. First, the militia had turned out promptly and conducted themselves aggressively, causing serious annoyance to the enemy throughout their march. Alexander deserves some credit for this, and so do Knyphausen and his British and Loyalist colleagues for provoking the Americans to a frenzy of rage in the series of raids over the winter and spring, and the burning of Connecticut Farms. Colonel Dayton and Lieutenant Colonel Smith with their detachment conducted themselves particularly well at the defile and in the subsequent retreat through Connecticut Farms, sapping substantial momentum from the enemy. Maxwell also deserves some credit, but how much is unclear; he was in overall command, but his actual contribution to the battle's tactical conduct seems not to have been substantial.

By the time Washington arrived on the field of battle, there was little for him to do. His conduct, though, is revealing and entirely in character considering his state of mind at this point in the war. Although he professed bafflement at Knyphausen's attack, Washington recognized that his army was fundamentally weak. His task at Connecticut Farms was to project strength for consumption by the enemy and the American public while taking every precaution not to push his chances too far and risk disaster. Gibbs's "attack" with the commander in chief's guard late in the afternoon of June 7 was little more than a piece of showmanship. Hand's subsequent attack on the morning of June 8, albeit provoked by rage and not directly approved by Washington, was of much the same character. Neither attack was pushed with determination, for the simple reason that the risks far outweighed any potential benefits.

In the wake of the battle, American soldiers and civilians celebrated their own bravery while steaming over enemy atrocities, which was just as Washington wished. "Never did troops either Continental or militia behave better, than ours did," Maxwell crowed to Governor Livingston. "[E]very one that had an opportunity, (which they mostly all had) vied with each other who could serve the country most." Deep down, though, Washington suspected that his army remained very shaky indeed.[39]

The consequences on the other side were wholly negative. Knyphausen admitted he had "found the disposition of the inhabitants by no means such as I expected, on the contrary they were everywhere in arms, nor did I find that spirit of desertion amongst their troops which it was represented to me existed amongst them." Clinton was annoyed when he learned about the venture, dubbing it "ill-timed" and "malapropos," and Knyphausen earned little credit among his own officers and men. Worse, he and many other British and German officers concluded they had been duped by loyal American officials such as Tryon, Major General Robertson, and Franklin—"Quondam Governors," and "Lawyers better skill'd in Quirks than sound, disinterested Views," as Deputy Quartermaster General Archibald Robertson called them. Loyalists in New York, for their part, were "vexed," blaming Wurmb and Knyphausen for failing to push their advantage. It was just one more wedge of distrust separating King George III's military leaders from the Americans they had supposedly come to defend.[40]

The British occupied New York City in August 1776 and would remain until the end of the war in 1783. The British made forays outside the city on a number of occasions to attempt to draw George Washington's army into battle, while Washington contemplated trapping the British forces in the city in 1779–1780 with a joint French and American operation. (*Library of Congress*)

British commander Henry Clinton and his army sailed for Charleston, South Carolina, in December 1779, and lay siege to the city. After it had fallen, Clinton returned to New York in June 1780 and prepared to attack the Americans in northern New Jersey. (*New York Public Library*)

Sir Henry Clinton was appointed commander-in-chief for North America in 1778 and held the position until after the siege of Yorktown. (*National Army Museum*)

General Wilhelm von Knyphausen led British and Hessian forces in the Battle for Connecticut Farms, New Jersey, while Clinton was in South Carolina. (*New York Public Library*)

General Nathanael Greene made a critical maneuver at the Battle of Springfield, New Jersey, that helped stop the British advance. (*National Park Service*)

General William Alexander, who styled himself "Lord Stirling," commanded Continental and militia troops in northern New Jersey, including those that fought in both the battles of Connecticut Farms and Springfield. (*New York Public Library*)

Marquis de Lafayette commanded the Connecticut division prior to the Battle of Connecticut Farms. (*New York Public Library*)

Colonel Elias Dayton commanded Continental and militia soldiers with distinction at the battles of Connecticut Farms and Springfield. (*New York Public Library*)

General Jedediah Huntington temporarily commanded Continental forces in Lafayette's absence. (*New York Public Library*)

George Washington organized the successful defense against the two British attacks designed to defeat his army in 1780. (*Metropolitan Museum of Art*)

"Liberty Hall," New Jersey governor William Livingston's mansion was about two miles northwest of Connecticut Farms. Livingston fled the mansion in order not to be captured as the British and Hessians overwhelmed the village, but his wife and family remained and were not harmed. (*New York Public Library*)

An American rifleman, left, and Continental soldier, right. (*Anne S. K. Brown Military Collection, Brown University Library*)

A British grenadier sketched in 1778. (*Anne S. K. Brown Military Collection, Brown University Library*)

American soldiers in combat sketched by John Singleton Copely in 1795. Copely left America before the Revolution, but this recreation provides an idea of the intimacy of close quarters fighting such as that at Connecticut Farms and Springfield. (*Anne S. K. Brown Military Collection, Brown University Library*)

American light cavalry. (*Anne S. K. Brown Military Collection, Brown University Library*)

Jäger corps illustrated in 1784 by J.C. Muller in green coats. From left to right, an officer with a sword, a rifleman, a musician with a hunting horn, and another rifleman. (*Anne S. K. Brown Military Collection, Brown University Library*)

This late eighteenth-century illustration is reminiscent of the farmland surrounding Connecticut Farms that gave way to Morristown, New Jersey, and the Short Hills in the distance. (*Library of Congress*)

THREE

Clinton Arrives

THERE NOW COMMENCED A PERIOD of exceptional tension and un-certainty. In New York, Knyphausen must have awaited Clinton's arrival with trepidation, expecting possibly a berating but also quick action. The British and German troops at Elizabethtown Point and on Staten Island worked to reorganize, keep vigilant watch on the enemy, and prepare for another incursion in a cam-paigning season that had barely begun. On shipboard, passing up the coast of the Carolinas and Virginia and on to New York, Clinton wondered what he would find awaiting him and prepared to move accordingly. His own troops were flush with the victory at Charleston but knew that bigger challenges awaited them.

Washington, meanwhile, was practically frantic with worry. Everywhere he looked he saw weakness: sorely understrength Continental units that still were not filling up with new enlist-ments, militiamen who thought they had done their jobs and were eager to return home, inadequate supplies, want of cavalry, and field leadership of uncertain quality. He could only address these in bits and pieces, and all in an atmosphere of uncertainty about what the enemy would do next.

Cavalry was a first priority, for Washington saw it as vital to fend off enemy raids and, more important, to provide quick intelligence of enemy movements. His thoughts turned immediately to Lee's legion, which he had fortunately resisted sending south. On June 8, Washington wrote to the Board of War, asking it to send the legion to join the main army. Cavalry was "infinitely wanted," he explained, for the enemy had "a considerable body of Horse which we want Horse to counteract, and we want them besides for the purpose of reconoitring." Three days later, Lee wrote to Washington, reporting that he was then at Scotch Plains with his cavalry—the infantry under Captain Allen McLane was already in Virginia and would not return until late in the summer—and that he would arrive in Springfield the same evening.

After giving the horses a brief rest and conferring with Washington on the morning of June 12, Lee and his "beautiful corps of light-horse, the men in complete uniform, and the horses very elegant and finely disciplined," rode off to join the advance guard, where they were met by a small infantry detachment—apparently part of Gibbs's command—provided to replace the missing McLane. Meanwhile, Washington recalled Colonel Stephen Moylan's 4th Continental Dragoons from winter camp in Connecticut, called the Philadelphia Light Horse to camp, and ordered Brigadier General Nathaniel Heard to send small parties of mounted New Jersey militia to patrol the roads on either flank, paying particular attention to the southern route through Scotch Plains to Morristown along which Lee's horsemen were approaching.[1]

Washington also needed somebody he could rely on to command the advance guard—and that, apparently, was not Major General Alexander. That individual, for reasons that now remain unclear, had been a somewhat distant figure during the Connecticut Farms episode, drifting in and out of the picture and never clearly in command control. Too much was at stake for that to continue. On June 9, then, the commander in chief appointed Major General Steuben to command the advance guard consisting of the New Jersey Brigade, Major Gibbs's detachment (Hand's command having been reabsorbed), and the advance militia. Washington carefully directed Heard and his militia to take orders from Steuben and not Alexander, who was shifted to command the second line.[2]

With cavalry on the way and a man he could trust commanding the advance guard, Washington placed his camp under tight security—any "transient persons" passing through camp were to be immediately arrested—established a signals protocol so the troops would come immediately under arms in case of alarm, and carefully distributed the 2,840 militiamen estimated to have arrived by this time, either in guard posts or in attachments to Continental units. No doubt exhaling a deep sigh, he then sat down at his headquarters in Jacob Briant's house in Springfield to consider enemy intentions and his own next moves.[3]

The more he thought about Connecticut Farms, the less conclusive it seemed. The New Jersey Brigade had done well—Washington rightly singled out Dayton for praise—and so had the militia. Yet "perseverance," Washington knew, was not in the militia's repertoire The enemy, for all he knew, was simply waiting for the Americans to get tired and go home. And yet even with that in mind, he had no choice but to send home half, or about 1,500 of the currently assembled militia, lest they refuse to turn out in another emergency. As for the Continentals, as currently constituted they were "totally inadequate to our safety." From this perspective, Connecticut Farms looked not like a victory redolent of untapped strength but like a near-run escape. Had Knyphausen pushed harder, Washington believed, "Our heavy Cannon and stores would inevitably have fallen into their hands, as our military force was incompetent to their protection and the means of conveying them to places more distant, for want of horses & Carriages out of our power."[4]

Never a man to underestimate his enemy, Washington could not bring himself to believe that Knyphausen had really been defeated at Connecticut Farms. If he had failed to push hard, it must be because he had only intended an "amusement," or feint, to pin Washington's army down in New Jersey while the real effort was directed elsewhere. Why else would Knyphausen's forces still be hanging around Elizabethtown Point—scouts even detected small reinforcements—rather than having withdrawn totally to Staten Island?[5]

By June 10, Washington had convinced himself that the real enemy effort would be directed against West Point, just as soon as Lieutenant General Henry Clinton returned from Charleston with his army. On that date he wrote urgently to his own Brigadier General James Clinton to pull his brigade out of Albany and move as quickly as possible to reinforce Major General Robert Howe's garrison at West Point. On the same day, he wrote to Howe urging vigilance and telling him to begin preparing supplies for a possible siege. "In either case the most disastrous consequences are to be apprehended," he told the camp committee. Despairing of adequate numerical strength or supplies to hold anywhere, he suggested to the committee that as soon as Henry Clinton arrived, which could be any moment, the commander in chief would "in all probability be obliged to retire beyond the Delaware, and leave the fortresses in the highlands of New York to be defended as well as they may be by the present weak and inadequate garrison, as he has no prospect of supplying an additional number of troops at that post, for the want of flour." While he would soon abandon this desperate idea, it is probably no coincidence that Martha Washington departed Morristown at this time for the relative safety of Mount Vernon. Her husband almost certainly ordered her to go.[6]

The ugly truth was that there was little Washington could do. He could, and did, exhort the states to fill up their Continental quotas—but that process could take months. He could, and did, scour the country for supplies for his own army and for West Point. He drew up a detailed plan for calling out and rallying the New Jersey militia in case of emergency and flattered them by proclaiming that any militiaman injured at Connecticut Farms could elect to receive treatment in Continental hospitals "to effect their recovery from the wounds which they have acquired with so much Honor to themselves and to their Country." Washington even suggested that Howe—who by this time had also grown convinced that an attack on West Point was imminent and offered the enemy an "easy conquest"—send spies into New York to mislead the enemy into thinking the Americans were preparing an attack on Fort Washington or some other post. But these measures, Washington knew, amounted to little in the aggregate.[7]

Lee, at least, was seeing some action rather than just watching and waiting, but that hardly made him feel any better. For several days, his cavalry patrolled aggressively around Elizabethtown, skirmishing occasionally, and on June 13 he clashed with a probe by British dragoons and mounted jäger above the stone bridge over the Elizabeth River. This steady raiding and counterraiding around Elizabethtown continued for many days, producing an enervating effect on both sides. American militia fired constantly on Knyphausen's outposts, shooting horses when they couldn't hit men and even wounding a British engineer, Lieutenant John Hills, as he sketched a map of the June 8 fracas at Elizabethtown Point.[8]

More generally, though, Lee noticed to his dismay that militia were deserting their posts in increasing numbers. Washington's subsequent decision to recall Gibbs's detachment from the advance party, replacing it with a less reliable detachment under Major James Parr, did not sit well with Lee, for whom the call for good infantry became a mantra until McLane rejoined him. Even so, Lee captured a patrol of seven men of the 43rd Regiment of Foot on June 16. On the following day he carried out, at Steuben's orders, a raid against Elizabethtown, where Knyphausen's troops had constructed two redoubts commanding the main road. Lee claimed that his raid threw the enemy into "general consternation." Knyphausen, by contrast, reported mockingly that the Americans merely brought up a single artillery piece to the stone bridge at midnight, fired a few rounds at the Donop Regiment (knocking its colonel's swagger stick out of his hand), and then fled into the darkness. In any event, Lee continued aggressive skirmishing and intelligence gathering over the days that followed.[9]

The dreaded news of Henry Clinton's arrival with his army on board Admiral Arbuthnot's fleet at Sandy Hook, New Jersey, came on June 17 in the form of a letter from Colonel David Forman, who had established observation posts all along the Jersey shore. Washington reacted as if to an electric shock. On the same day, he wrote to volunteer Francis Van Dyke, instructing him to have spies in New York garner intelligence of the enemy's intentions at the earliest possible opportunity. Next he wrote to Major General Howe at West Point, urging immediate preparations for the defense of that post and the calling in of all available militia and state regiments. "The movements of the enemy will probably be rapid and a correspondent spirit of energy should animate our efforts," Washington told him. To President of Congress Samuel Huntington, Washington exhorted, "there is no time to be lost— The danger is imminent and pressing—The obstacles to be surmounted are great and numerous—and our efforts must be instant, unreserved and universal."[10]

Others did their best to assist in the work of preparedness, including New York politician and former general Philip Schuyler, who worked as an intermediary with Congress and the states to get Washington's needs met; and patriotic Pennsylvania financier Robert Morris, who spent his own money lavishly to secure rations for the troops. But preparedness against what? Scouts informed Washington, correctly, that the enemy was reinforcing its fortifications at Elizabethtown Point and building a pontoon bridge from there to Staten Island. "The bridge was the best of the kind I ever saw," recorded Lieutenant George Mathew. "There were very large planks laid across sloops, and wide enough for five or six men to march abreast." The British also constructed and reinforced redoubts around the landing.[11]

Lee, still skirmishing and scouting actively, reported that two enemy regiments had been moved into Elizabethtown Point, while other reports had Clinton and four thousand additional troops landed on Staten Island and moving to ferries opposite Perth Amboy. On June 19, Clinton appeared at Elizabethtown Point to review the troops. Yet Lee, Howe, and Washington became increasingly convinced that the real enemy object was West Point. Anticipating the same thing, Steuben wrote to Washington on June 20 asking to be reassigned from the advance corps to West Point—and the commander in chief promptly complied.[12]

Washington's focus on West Point amounted to little more than an educated guess, based on his perception of that post's importance to the larger cause. Late on June 20, he came up with a plan. The advance corps, now commanded by Greene and consisting of Maxwell's and Stark's brigades along with Lee's cavalry and some militia, about three thousand men in all, would hold in place to guard the approaches to Morristown—but with wide discretion to act as Greene saw fit under any circumstances. Meanwhile, the Connecticut and Pennsylvania brigades, about 2,500 Continentals under Brigadier General Jedediah Huntington (temporarily commanding in Lafayette's absence) and Major General Arthur St. Clair, would march toward Pompton but stop ten miles north of Morristown at Rockaway Bridge. From that position they would still be within range to move back to Springfield or Morristown if necessary, while also being situated for a quick move toward West Point. This move began on the afternoon of June 21, while Washington settled his affairs in Springfield. By the following morning he was at Rockaway Bridge, and by June 23 his entire detachment had arrived there with him.[13]

INTELLIGENCE OF CLINTON'S INTENTIONS remained unclear in part because the British commander was unsure himself. Though fresh from his crushing victory at Charleston, he found little in New York to please him. He later claimed to have initially planned to carry out a "coup de main" against Washington by launching two columns—one under Knyphausen from Elizabethtown Point and the other under himself from Perth Amboy—and leaving Washington unable to attack one without leaving himself vulnerable to the other. This was the gist of the plan he had told Crosbie to "hint" to Knyphausen earlier in the month. By this means there was every reason to hope the British could smash through to Morristown, capturing Washington's supplies and ordnance there and scattering his army. This would prevent the French and Americans from working in concert and possibly lead to "a general submission of the whole continent." Had Washington known of this plan, he probably would have agreed both with its prospects for success and likely consequences.[14]

Knyphausen's attack of June 7, however, had transformed previously somnolent eastern New Jersey into an angry hornet's nest and also worn down the British and German troops. Those at Elizabethtown Point were not having an easy time of it, having to deal with frequent raids and harassment while hemmed into a narrow neck of land without tents, so that even their enemies pitied them. Clinton, a sour-tempered man at the best of times, stewed over this "very unpleasant and mortifying situation" until he could barely stand Knyphausen's presence. Just before landing on Staten Island, though, Clinton received letters from the traitor Benedict Arnold with significant and promising intelligence. Arnold had learned correctly that Rochambeau's fleet was bound not for New York but Newport, Rhode Island. Moreover, West Point's garrison had become so weak from lack of supplies that Washington was even more sensitive than usual to its defense. While Clinton did not view a siege of that post as feasible given Rochambeau's arrival, American fears for West Point suggested the possibility of drawing Washington into a trap.[15]

With this in mind, Clinton reacted quickly to intelligence that arrived June 22, indicating that Washington had divided his army. Moving rapidly before the French could get established in Rhode Island and menace his rear, Clinton sent the Queen's Rangers to Elizabethtown Point. He also ordered Major General Mathew, "supported by" Knyphausen, to attack with six thousand troops toward Springfield—not evidently with a view to capturing that place but in order to slow down Washington's move north. Clinton then intended to proceed up the Hudson with his remaining four thousand men under Major General Alexander Leslie to Haverstraw Bay, and disembark on the river's west bank. In so doing he would drive a wedge between Washington and West Point while keeping New York City well protected. As in Clinton's earlier plan, Washington would be caught between two fires— this time on a larger scale. If he did nothing, he could be defeated in detail; if he moved against either Mathew/Knyphausen or Clinton, he might leave himself vulnerable to attack by the other.[16]

Clinton's plan assumed that the American advance guard— now a rearguard—at Elizabethtown would be weak, which was certainly true. Now, though, that force was led by the formidable Nathanael Greene, who spent the night of June 22–23 struggling to reconcile conflicting intelligence. Even as the commander in chief prepared his move, a spy from Elizabethtown informed Greene that the British were fully aware of the American movements, and that Clinton planned to move on Smith's Clove to cut Washington off from West Point. Just as soon as he dispatched this intelligence to Washington, however, Greene had second thoughts. His spy seemed shady—what if he was in fact a double agent who was just trying to lure Washington north so the British could strike toward the vital provision depot at Trenton? Greene forwarded these doubts to a probably now thoroughly befuddled Washington.

Lee, meanwhile, scouted actively around Elizabethtown but remained certain that Clinton was preparing to embark for a direct assault on West Point. On the evening of June 22, a small force of Queen's Rangers and jäger raided an American infantry outpost at Elizabethtown with the hope of capturing a few prisoners for interrogation. This they accomplished, but at the cost of two men killed, several wounded, and two "drunk and sulky" stragglers whom the Americans captured. Little did anyone know that this brief encounter marked the opening shots of the Battle of Springfield.[17]

FOUR

The Battle of Springfield, June 23, 1780

As HE PREPARED HIS FORCES to attack in the early morning hours of June 23, Knyphausen must have sensed an opportunity for redemption. Although he could not count on the element of surprise, he did have a number of advantages not available on June 7. First and foremost, his lead division under Major General Mathew was already ensconced in New Jersey, with its forward elements in Elizabethtown, which had become more or less of a no-man's-land over the preceding days. Those still on Staten Island, meanwhile, could cross quickly over on the pontoon bridge, thus avoiding the delays that had plagued his crossing on June 7.

Knyphausen's available forces once again amounted to some six thousand men, arrayed this time in three divisions. Mathew, advancing with the 1st Division as per Clinton's specific orders, had the Queen's Rangers, the 1st and 4th Battalions of the Loyalist New Jersey Volunteers, the British Guards, the Landgraf Regiment, and cavalry of the British 17th Dragoons, the Loyalist

Staten Island Dragoons, and Captain Friedrich Diemar's Hussars (a curious unit made up of escaped German prisoners of war from Saratoga). Knyphausen commanded the 2nd Division, which included the Jäger Corps; the British 37th, 38th, and 57th Regiments of Foot; the Leib, Bose, and Bayreuth Regiments; and a detachment of the 17th Dragoons. Fifteen to twenty artillery pieces were distributed between these two divisions. The 3rd Division—commanded by Robertson and consisting of the 22nd and 43rd Regiments of Foot; the Anspach, Donop, and Bünau Regiments; and a company of the 17th Regiment of Foot—was to remain at Elizabethtown Point to operate as a reserve and protect Knyphausen's line of retreat, supply, and communications against militia.[1]

Knyphausen, perhaps under Clinton's instructions, devised a more devious plan of attack than he had used on June 7. Mathew's division, led by the Queen's Rangers and New Jersey Volunteers, would head the initial attack before dawn on June 23. This time, however, instead of just trying to punch through toward Springfield, the column would divide at Connecticut Farms. After clearing out any American resistance there, Mathew's troops would swing to the right, march northeast about half a mile along a connecting road, and then turn west again to advance rapidly down the Vauxhall Road. Knyphausen would meanwhile push directly down the Galloping Hill Road as he had two weeks earlier. Attempting to defend both approaches might well stretch the Americans past the breaking point.[2]

Simcoe's rangers led the advance at about 4:00 AM, flanked by the volunteers and followed by the rest of Mathew's division. Knyphausen's division departed at 4:30 AM. Kept on their toes by Washington and Greene, and well-led on point, the Americans responded crisply. Lee, Dayton, and the militia fell back quickly, exchanging only a few shots with the fast-moving enemy as their column passed Liberty Hall. Maxwell, at Connecticut Farms, passed the alert on to Greene at Bryant's Tavern behind Springfield. Greene ordered Stark's brigade to stand to arms, notified Washington at six o'clock that "The Enemy are out, and on their march towards this place in full force," and took stock of the situation.

Assuming that Knyphausen intended to flank him, Greene disposed his troops accordingly. Ordering the battered New Jersey Brigade to fight for the ruins of Connecticut Farms would be pointless. Instead, while Dayton and the militia prepared a rearguard action in that settlement, Greene detached Colonel Ogden's 1st New Jersey Regiment and sent it with Lee's Dragoons and some militia to take post in the Short Hills behind Little's Bridge about one and a half miles north of Springfield on the Vauxhall Road, thus protecting his vulnerable left flank.

Nor did Greene intend to hold Springfield, which possessed no intrinsic military value.

Like Connecticut Farms, Springfield was also an appendage of Elizabethtown, although slightly larger with some thirty residences. Its Presbyterian church had a considerable congregation, and some of the homes were substantial. Yet Springfield was basically similar to its now burned-out neighbor to the immediate east. It was also a village of prosperous middling yeomen, and it shared the fertile soil and generally level terrain of Connecticut Farms.[3]

Not far beyond the town, however, the landscape changed. To the northwest the Short Hills rose gently, while to the west the first range of the Watchung Mountains climbed more abruptly. Springfield lay between branches of the Rahway River, and bridges over the Rahway controlled access to the village. Wooden spans on the Galloping Hill and Vauxhall Roads respectively fronted the eastern approach to the village and provided entrance from the north. Another bridge led west toward the Watchungs. The river was fordable, but the bridges at least offered better defensive points than anything in Connecticut Farms. Another difference lay in the fact that Springfield was a road junction. From the village center well-established roads led north, south, east, and west—and the route west led directly to Hobart Gap, only some three miles away. In effect, Springfield was the gateway to the gap, and the town was valuable to Greene only to the extent that any fighting there might prevent Knyphausen from breaking through to the west.

Instead of planning a final stand in front of the town, Greene deployed Colonel Israel Angell's 2nd Rhode Island from Stark's brigade and some small detachments with a field piece to hold the bridge over the Rahway (from which they removed the planks) long enough to cover Dayton's retreat. Behind the village, Shreve's 2nd New Jersey Regiment would wait with some of Thomas Procter's artillery under the command of Lieutenant Colonel Thomas Forrest. Their role was to hold the door open for Dayton and Angell to pull back from the village and across a second bridge over another branch of the Rahway. Stark's brigade, with Spencer's badly weakened regiment and militia, remained in reserve as Greene retained the bulk of his forces to move as circumstances dictated. Engagements at Springfield would be delaying actions only; the key thing was to hold on to Hobart Gap.[4]

Dayton had little hope of holding out in Connecticut Farms for long. Nevertheless, he stationed his weak regiment at the same defile he had defended on June 7, where the Galloping Hill Road proceeded through a hollow over the high ground in Connecticut Farms. Some of his Continentals took post in an orchard on his left, and others in a thicket on his right—able to support each other but with clear lines of retreat.

The Loyalist advance guard soon came into contact with this position and handled it smartly. While the flanking volunteers engaged the Continentals in the orchard and the thicket, Simcoe formed his rangers into column and sent them in quick march along the road through the center of the hollow. They then wheeled right into the orchard and quickly broke the American position there. But Dayton also had his men well drilled. Though Simcoe moved in swift pursuit, scattering the Continentals in the orchard but only taking a few prisoners, he was unable to cut off either detachment from the bridge, which they reached and crossed in safety under cover of Angell's cannon, apparently retiring to the vicinity of a mill behind Springfield.[5]

The artillery piece accompanying Angell's Rhode Islanders opened fire on the Loyalists as they observed the American position from the heights above the bridge. At 6:30 AM, Washington heard this fire, in which two Loyalists were killed. Mathew waited in Connecticut Farms until Knyphausen arrived about 8:00 AM, at which time they decided to execute their flanking maneuver. Pulling back the Loyalists, Mathew turned his division north and set course for the Vauxhall Road and Little's Bridge. Knyphausen, meanwhile, moved forward in a leisurely manner to the high ground overlooking the bridge in front of Springfield. There, with great ostentation, he deployed a battery of several guns that engaged Angell's single gun in an inconclusive artillery duel. In so doing, the German general hoped to fix Greene's attention while his flank was turned. He and the English general had agreed that Knyphausen would attack the bridge once Mathew "had attained his object, or had met with much opposition."[6]

Lee and Ogden, meanwhile, took up defensive positions that Greene had likely already prescribed for them. Vauxhall Bridge, a little over a mile northeast of Angell's position farther up the east branch of the Rahway, was easily flanked and suitable only as an advance post. Lee merely stationed some militia there, possibly with a leavening of a few Continentals. He placed his main force somewhat over a mile farther west, behind Little's Bridge over the west branch of the Rahway. Here Ogden's two hundred or so Continentals and Lee's dragoons, dismounted of course, could take advantage of some rougher terrain in the approaches to the Short Hills to the southwest of Newark Mountain. Although Lee's exact dispositions are now hard to determine, it appears he used militia and a detachment of infantry under Captain George Walker as pickets, placing them in thickets along the river, with his main body of infantry some distance behind.[7]

Simcoe moved well in advance of the slower-marching British infantry, and Mathew appears to have kept his cavalry in reserve. Halting at Vauxhall Bridge, the Loyalists amused themselves for a time by unlimbering their light fieldpieces and taking potshots at "small parties of the enemy scattered up and down in the fields and woods." As soon as Simcoe heard the cannonading begin from Knyphausen's forces before the Springfield bridge—the timing is uncertain but it may have been about 9:00 AM—the Loyalists crossed the Vauxhall Bridge without opposition and proceeded west until they reached Little's Bridge. There, Simcoe observed, the Americans behind the bridge, "possessing the heights, seemed to be drawn up in small bodies by echelon, so as to concentre their fire upon the road."

What happened next in this contest of two superb field officers is open to interpretation. Simcoe, in a somewhat confused account, describes approaching the bridge in column, deploying into line and then extending it. First dispatching a small party under a Lieutenant Shaw to clear out some American "riflemen" (more likely musket-bearing militia and Walker's Continentals) who covered the Rahway riverbed from some thickets, Simcoe then crossed the river. Lee's troops fought back—Knyphausen heard a "loud roar of guns" to his right at 11:00 AM—but were soon outflanked on their left and undertook a hasty but ordered retreat. Greene explains that "by fording the river and gaining the point of the hill they obliged the Major with his party to give up the pass." Instead of pushing onward, however, the Loyalist regiments skirmished for a short time before pulling back to rejoin Mathew with his column on the road behind them.

Greene later reported to Washington that Lee had fought at Little's Bridge "with great obstinacy, and the enemy must have received very considerable injury." Major General Alexander likewise described the affair as "well disputed," although casualty returns show that neither Lee (one killed, four wounded), nor Simcoe (two killed, seven wounded) suffered significant casualties over the course of the battle. Greene, understandably overreacting to Simcoe's thrust, decided at 11:00 AM that Mathew was pushing on into the Short Hills, and moved his own forces back accordingly to cover the Hobart Gap while dispatching two regiments to support Lee.[8]

Although Lee had to pull back some distance farther into the hills, there was in fact little real danger. Discovering the American

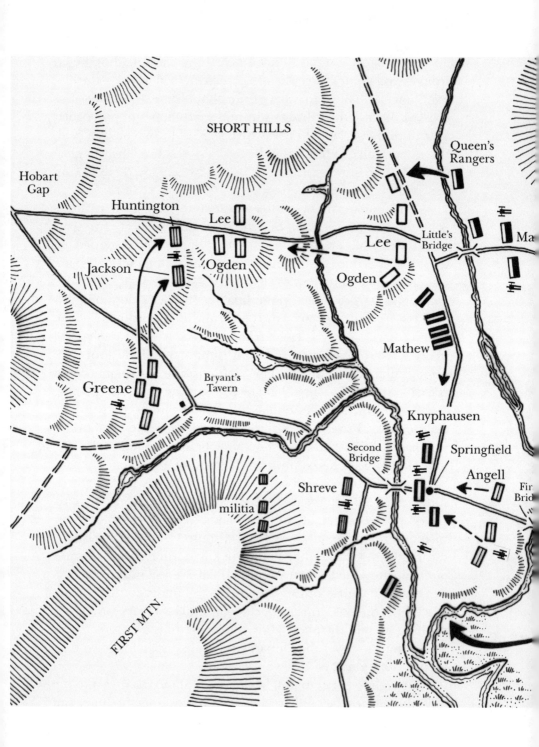

SHORT HILLS

Queen's
Rangers

Hobart
Gap

Huntington

Lee

Lee

Little's
Bridge

Ma

Jackson

Ogden

Ogden

Mathew

Greene

Bryant's
Tavern

Knyphausen

Second
Bridge

Springfield

Angell

Shreve

Fir
Brid

militia

FIRST MTN.

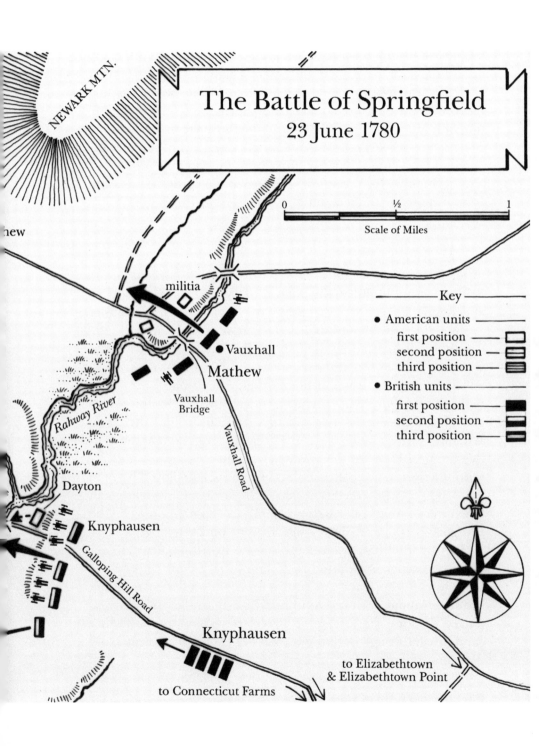

The Battle of Springfield
23 June 1780

NEWARK MTN.

hew

militia

Vauxhall

Mathew

Vauxhall
Bridge

Rahway River

Vauxhall Road

Dayton

Knyphausen

Galloping Hill Road

Knyphausen

to Connecticut Farms

to Elizabethtown
& Elizabethtown Point

0   ½   1
Scale of Miles

Key

• American units
  first position
  second position
  third position
• British units
  first position
  second position
  third position

infantry drawn up in apparent strength in the hills behind yet another branch of the Rahway and still blocking the route to Hobart Gap, the casualty-averse Mathew paused for a time before sending his troops south on the direct road to Springfield with the intention of reuniting the two columns in the town. He may have done so on earlier instructions from Knyphausen, who had already been told by Clinton that his effort amounted to little more than a feint. In any event, Mathew withdrew under growing pressure from American militia coming in from the north.[9]

WHEN SIMCOE BEGAN HIS ACTION to drive off Lee's force at Little's Bridge around 11:00 AM, Knyphausen deployed his own troops to attack Angell's regiment defending the deplanked bridge before Springfield. This bloody affair lasted about forty minutes, as the Continentals, backed by their single fieldpiece commanded by Captain Thomas Thompson, presented "very obstinate resistance." During the initial artillery duel, Angell had kept his infantry posted in some orchards near Springfield for safety, although some British shells landed in and around the town. When the British infantry—casualty figures suggest that the 37th Regiment of Foot led the advance—began moving downhill toward the river in two columns, however, Angell deployed his men forward to take post on either side of the bridge. Ensign Jeremiah Greenman thought the Rahway here was "pasable onley by the Bridge as it appear'd Slowey and Swampy on Each Side."[10]

The Continentals opened fire on the British infantry as they came into range, supported by Thompson's fieldpiece on a rise to their rear. The American musket and cannon fire "played very briskly on them," but concentrated British artillery fire soon silenced the lone cannon and its brave crew (Thompson, hit by a cannonball through both thighs, was evacuated to a hospital and died later that day).

While the rival forces exchanged fire, a civilian drama played out unnoticed (or at least unmentioned) by the soldiery of either side. When the British first approached Springfield, most residents responded predictably. Like their Connecticut Farms neighbors, they hid their valuables and fled west or to the nearby Short Hills. But one family was late getting away, so the story goes, and when the fight at the bridge erupted, they found themselves caught between the British and the Americans. Escape over the bridge, the family's original goal, obviously was out of the question. Making for a patch of woods, in the excitement of the moment the parents and two children became separated. A desperate fourteen-year-old girl, with her baby sister in her arms, then managed to ford the Rahway while the battle raged. Running through the village, her parents found her on a road outside of town. The family reached safety in the Short Hills.[11]

The lucky teenager was not the only one fording the river. As the British infantry concentrated their fire on Angell's men, jäger waded the Rahway, only three or four feet deep, on either side and outflanked the Rhode Islanders. For the Continentals, the game at the bridge was up; the advancing Germans left them no choice but to abandon the bridge.[12]

The Americans pulled back in good order and conducted a fighting retreat through the village and nearby orchards from point to point. Captain Stephen Olney, commanding one platoon, remembered the fighting being so close that "the wind of their balls would at times shake the hair of my head"; eventually he was wounded in the arm. A piece of local lore—popularized by Washington Irving and now impossible to prove or disprove—has the grieving Rev. James Caldwell passing out Watts's hymn books from the church to Angell's soldiers to use as wadding for their muskets and crying, "Give 'em Watts, boys!" Battered but uncowed, Angell's men finally withdrew with the intention of passing behind Shreve's regiment at the second bridge.[13]

All was not well with the New Jersey Brigade, however, if the subsequent testimony of Lieutenant Colonel William Stephens Smith is to be believed. As the troops were called to arms on the morning of June 23, Shreve detained Smith. "He laid his hand upon my shoulder," Smith later told Washington, "and said he wish'd me to take charge of his regiment that day, that it would probably prove a warm one and as I had youth and activity upon my side I could continue with the regiment let their situation be what it would[;] as for himself he was a heavy man and should the regiment be press'd he should be obliged [to] leave it." Smith said he would be happy to do so with the consent of Shreve's officers. The colonel replied that they would welcome the command change "and was confident if we came to action they would do me honour and desired me to take good care of them."

There was nothing in Israel Shreve's background to account for his alleged behavior. Born to Quaker stock, he was a prominent and prosperous farmer, justice of the peace, and militia officer from Burlington County in southern New Jersey. An early patriot, as a lieutenant colonel of the 2nd New Jersey Regiment he fought in Canada in 1776. He then led the regiment in grueling retreat to Fort Ticonderoga. As colonel of the 2nd, Shreve served in the 1777 campaign (he was wounded at Brandywine); and while most of the army wintered at Valley Forge, the 2nd fenced with British probes in southern New Jersey. Later in 1778, Shreve helped harass the British march across the state in the Monmouth campaign, and he served creditably in the Sullivan Expedition of 1779. The man was a tested veteran, and Smith's claim that Shreve avoided action because "he was a heavy man" (which admittedly he was) seems dubious in view of his combat record.

Whatever Shreve's motives, after a few formalities the changeover was effected amiably enough, and Smith led the regiment toward and over the second bridge behind Springfield, where they joined some of Lieutenant Colonel Forrest's artillery. Shreve accompanied Smith briefly and then rode away. The troops remained there until Angell's regiment began losing hold of its position at the first bridge, whereupon Greene ordered the artillery to deploy on high ground near the Presbyterian Church overlooking a crossroads. When the guns completed their move, Greene ordered Smith to move his regiment forward and deploy "upon the left of the Brigade [presumably Dayton's regiment, withdrawn from Connecticut Farms] which then lay on the right of the mill in rear of the town."

Conflicting orders now arrived, suggesting some uncertainty on Greene's part about how to proceed. First, Brigade Major John Ross of the 2nd New Jersey handed Smith orders—from whom Smith did not later disclose—to march his regiment forward into Springfield and await further orders from Greene. As the troops began their move, however, Greene's aide-de-camp, Lieutenant Colonel Lewis Morris, rode up and, after receiving confirmation that Smith was commanding the regiment in Shreve's place, declared that Greene wanted him to pull back behind the second bridge and cover the retreat of Angell's regiment and Forrest's artillery, "for he expected they would be hard pressed." Presumably Dayton received similar orders.[14]

Smith carried out this move, occupying what he thought to be a secure position behind the bridge. Almost an hour passed, he claimed, until the first elements of Angell's hard-fighting Rhode Islanders appeared, carrying several wounded men. Angell arrived a few minutes later—probably around noon—and, after crossing a "morass" on Smith's right, rode up and asked for advice on where he should post his men. Smith recommended a knoll on his right to further secure that flank for a time before withdrawing, and Angell agreed. Shortly after the remaining American infantry and artillery pulled back behind the 2nd New Jersey, the first elements of the enemy arrived.[15]

Knyphausen's advance parties—presumably jäger—probed cautiously toward Smith's right, and after his troops in that sector fired a few volleys, he ordered them to cease fire. The Germans came closer and, as their shot continued "to fly briskly over us," Smith ordered his men to return the fire by platoons from right to left. Several volleys passed while Shreve skulked near a barn behind a nearby orchard—all that Smith could see was his horse's head. On the right, meanwhile, a small melee evidently developed in the area of a stone house where some men of Spencer's regiment and some militia had been posted, and the Americans threw back a sally by some of Knyphausen's troops.[16]

About half an hour passed before Shreve called for Smith, who found the colonel mounted on his horse behind a large apple tree. Shreve told Smith that his "right was in danger"—maybe referring to the trouble around the stone house—and then departed for the rear. One possible contributor to the colonel's withdrawal from the action—albeit not mentioned by Smith—was that Shreve's son John, a long-serving junior officer with the 2nd, was wounded during the fight while attempting to aid a wounded comrade. To give the elder Shreve the benefit of the doubt, his son's wounding would have constituted a significant distraction.[17]

With the artillery and Angell's men now withdrawn to safety, Smith ordered his regiment to cease fire and pull back. They wheeled to the left by platoons and marched back along the road toward the Short Hills. The enemy infantry did not press them but brought up some artillery pieces to shell the Americans and inflicted a few casualties—including a dragoon who was killed by a cannonball a short distance from Greene as he observed the withdrawal. Here, for all intents and purposes, the combat ended.[18]

Greene, meanwhile, had spent the morning monitoring events and fretting about the possibility of a strong push by the enemy column driving down the Vauxhall Road on his left. His headquarters were in Bryant's Tavern a mile west of Springfield, where the Galloping Hill Road began its ascent into the Short Hills—although as Smith's account suggests, he also spent much of the morning riding back and forth between there and Springfield. Stark's brigade, with leftovers from the New Jersey Brigade, were also held near Bryant's Tavern. Brigadier General Philemon Dickinson's militia, which did not come out in strength on this occasion, mostly hovered in the area south of Springfield, occasionally harassing Knyphausen's right.

Still without word from Lee by 11:00 AM but probably having heard the sound of firing from there, Greene imagined that Mathew might be pressing the Virginian through the Short Hills toward Chatham. He therefore took the precautionary measure of dispatching two regiments and a cannon to reinforce Lee, afterward pulling back Stark's brigade and the now-reunited New Jersey Brigade into the hills closer to Hobart's Gap. This placed the two wings of his force within easy supporting distance. The move was wise but unnecessary, for neither Mathew nor Knyphausen had any intention of pressing their attacks.[19]

Washington played even less of a role in the engagement than Greene. Word of Knyphausen's attack, and the sound of cannon fire, reached the commander in chief early that morning at Rockaway Bridge, and he sent his aide-de-camp, Major David Humphreys, to Springfield to investigate. Two more signal cannon—this time fired from camp—ordered the troops to prepare to move. Later that morning he threw his force into motion toward Springfield, with General Wayne's brigade in the van. Washington nevertheless remained well out of reach of Clinton, who later wrote that "that wary chief acted on this occasion with his usual caution, and by marching his army wide of the river contrived to place every part of it beyond our reach." Wayne's brigade arrived in support of Greene just behind the Hobart Gap by eight o'clock that evening. Washington had ordered stores evacuated from Morristown as a precautionary measure, but this also was unnecessary.[20]

Equally unnecessary were the events now unfolding in Springfield. After 11:00 AM, just as the fighting for the second bridge faded, several houses in Springfield burst into flames. "The burning of Springfield was against the positive orders of the commanding officers," wrote British Guards lieutenant George Mathew, who arrived on the scene later that afternoon, "but they found it impossible to keep the soldiers from setting fire to the houses." Major General Robertson claimed that the conflagration began when some British soldiers set fire to a house from which rebels had fired on them, and that some Loyalists took this as a signal to burn the whole place to the ground. The fact that British and Loyalist officers were at pains to disavow these burnings, instead of defending them as appropriate under the laws of war and military circumstances, again suggests that Knyphausen retained only a tenuous hold over his frustrated men.[21]

Major General Mathew's division rejoined Knyphausen in Springfield during the early afternoon, just after the last of Lieutenant Colonel Smith's column disappeared into the Short Hills. Knyphausen then ordered Mathew's troops to seize some nearby heights from which militia—possibly attempting to interfere with the burning of the town—were taking shots at his men. At 3:00 PM, judging the American positions (in Clinton's later words) "too respectable to encourage any further attempts," Knyphausen abandoned his expedition and pulled his force back toward Elizabethtown Point. The celerity of the movement, which took place in two columns, suggests that Knyphausen saw no hope of continuing effectively against opposition and that his purpose, to enact a feint in hopes of drawing out Washington where Clinton could get at him, had been effected. Some American deserters confirmed this impression by reporting that Washington had marched for West Point.[22]

Small parties of militia who entered Springfield on the heels of the departing enemy found the village already totally in flames and impossible to salvage aside from the residences of four local Loyalists that had been spared. A detachment of 120 men that Greene dispatched to harass Knyphausen's retreating columns could do no more than fling a few shots at their backs; nor was Stark's brigade, which followed up thereafter, able to catch up. Only Lee's cavalry managed to exchange some shots with Knyphausen's rearguard and capture the occasional straggler and abandoned supplies. By 7:00 PM, Knyphausen's entire force was safely ensconced at Elizabethtown Point and preparing to cross back to Staten Island. By sunrise the next day, they had completed their withdrawal and dismantled the pontoon bridge, leaving behind their fortifications to be demolished by the American militia.[23]

The whole affair had been, from the British point of view, a colossal waste of time and precious resources. Clinton, like Howe in the 1777 New Jersey campaign, had found Washington too canny to be drawn into the open for combat at a disadvantage. Nor had the Americans fallen to pieces before Knyphausen's two-pronged onslaught, although they had not been pushed very hard. Scrappy but undersupplied and outnumbered, the Americans had fallen back repeatedly before tactically well-executed enemy attacks. In doing so, though, they had succeeded in inflicting substantial casualties. And that, really, was the point. By this time, Knyphausen and to some extent Clinton lacked the will to accept significant losses in pursuit of Washington's army, and their tendency to cut bait quickly, just when the fighting seemed from the soldiers' eye view to be going their way, was intensely demoralizing for the British, German, and Loyalist troops under their command. On both occasions, they took out their frustration on the civilian inhabitants and their homes.

Casualties on the American side were light, tallied at fifteen killed, forty-nine wounded, and nine missing. British losses, Clinton confessed, were "rather more considerable than could have been well apprehended" and far greater than he could manage to lose. Knyphausen admitted to losing fourteen killed, eighty-nine wounded, and eleven missing, but a variety of American, British, and German sources suggest they may have lost up to a few dozen more, especially in missing. The Jäger Corps, once more in the thick of the fighting, endured a disproportionate share of these casualties—according to Ewald, fourteen killed and thirty-nine wounded in the Battle of Springfield (Knyphausen claimed they lost only one killed, fifteen wounded, and five missing).[24]

If the Americans accrued any benefit from the two battles it was the morale-boosting performance of their officers and men. Highest honors for June 23 should go to Colonels Angell and (once again) Dayton, as well as to Greene himself, who had effectively coordinated his defense with limited resources. Lee had also conducted himself efficiently, if without any special distinction. Washington, perhaps knowing that his primary duty was not to lose, had behaved with due caution. Only the militia, as Washington had predicted, failed to emerge in numbers sufficient to have a significant impact on the battlefield, except in harassing Mathew's column after it withdrew from Little's Bridge.

In burning Springfield, though, Knyphausen's troops had played into Washington's hands, once again (as with the torching of Connecticut Farms) providing a cause célèbre to galvanize Americans into resisting British savagery. "I am at a loss to determine what was the object of the enemy's expedition," Greene wrote Washington after Knyphausen's departure. "If it was to injure the troops under my command, or to penetrate further into the Country, they were frustrated. If it was the destruction of this place, it was a disgraceful one. I lament that our force was too small to save the town from ruin. I wish every American could have been a spectator, He would have felt for the sufferers and joined to revenge the injury." Greene also exhorted his troops to note the "savage-like" behavior of the "German boors" and their "satanic designs." It may be worth speculating whether any Americans who opened fire on the British from civilian residences did so with the specific intent of provoking retaliation.[25]

Clinton, who soon rejoined Knyphausen in New York City, had gambled and lost. By this point he had been fighting Washington for two years and should have known better than to expect the latter to make any stupid mistakes. Both Connecticut Farms and Springfield, in fact, may have had more to do with the competition of egos between Clinton and Knyphausen than with any clear conception of strategy. Simcoe and the troops under his command had conducted themselves quite well, showing once again that Loyalists could fight well if led effectively. Loyalist leaders in New York City, however, had failed to gain any credit, and the British and German soldiers' frustration with their leaders, their circumstances, and each other were becoming increasingly evident. With significant French land forces about to arrive in North America and with unhappy troops and limited military options, Clinton's position was becoming dangerous.

Conclusion

"THE GENERAL HAS OBSERVED with the highest satisfaction that the Behavior of the Troops upon every late occasion has exhibited signal proofs how much may be expected from their Valor improved as it now is by discipline, and affords the highest presage of Success in our future operations," Washington told his troops in general orders on June 26. Greene earned the commander in chief's specific praise for his battlefield leadership—and rightly so, for the Battle of Springfield may rightly be deemed Greene's victory. The militia at both battles, Washington told the president of Congress, "flew to arms universally and acted with a spirit equal to any thing I have seen in the course of the War."[1]

This was high praise indeed from a commander in chief who had long demonstrated skepticism about the militia, but no more than fair; by this point in the war, the average Jersey militiaman was no yokel but a battle-tested veteran. The performance of the militia had been impressive at Connecticut Farms and at least adequate at Springfield, marking a significant improvement from four years earlier. Thanks to the improved militia, and as these battles demonstrated, any royal penetration into the interior was bound to face resistance and incur casualties. Likewise the Continentals and militia, once bitter rivals who had on occasion fought each other as eagerly as they fought the enemy, had learned how to cooperate reasonably effectively on the field of battle.

These experiences may well have had an impact far beyond New Jersey. Springfield had been Nathanael Greene's first independent command, and he played a deft game. The Rhode Islander showed a clear understanding of key positions, of when and where to fight, and how long. At all times during the action at Springfield he kept his attention fixed on the one piece of really key terrain—Hobart Gap, the path through the Watchungs and the route to Morristown. Everything he did was calculated to prevent the British from reaching that pass. As events demonstrated, Greene was gifted with the ability to assess what was important and plan operations accordingly. It served him well when Washington sent him south to retrieve failing patriot fortunes there. Greene also appears to have balanced Continental and militia forces effectively, although the latter did not turn out on a very large scale at Springfield. He no doubt learned from the experience and applied the lessons on a larger scale in the South, making Springfield a preview of Greene's upcoming campaigns in the Carolinas.

Washington's correspondence for the next several weeks acquired a certain sense of creeping confidence, if not satisfaction (for he always feared complacency), in stark contrast to the near-panicked urgency that had characterized his letters in May and early June. Rochambeau's arrival in July at Newport rather than off New York City, thus crushing for a time Washington's cherished assault on the latter place, failed to discourage him. Far from what he had feared in the aftermath of the army's springtime travails and near mutiny, the troops at Morristown, and the people of New Jersey, had shown remarkable resilience. Time no longer looked on the verge of running out.

The Battles of Connecticut Farms and Springfield provided substantial clarity to the strategic situation in North America. Despite the hard winter at Morristown and the fall of Charleston, revolutionary fortunes waxed as British prospects waned. Washington could take his time to work out a plan for victory alongside Rochambeau's forces later in 1780 or even in 1781, instead of rushing to force a decision now. Clinton, by contrast, could not help but recognize the flagging morale of his forces in the mid-Atlantic. After Rochambeau's arrival at Newport forced the British commander to abandon plans for an attack on that place, he returned to the pessimistic and defensive mindset that he had displayed before the fall of Charleston. Instead of planning creatively for the future, he berated London for shortages of supplies and reinforcements, sneered at the Loyalists' false promises, and waited for Washington to attack him in New York. He even worried about assassination at the hands of enemy agents.[2]

Never had the king's soldiers been served more poorly by their generals. The British, German, and Loyalist American troops at Connecticut Farms and Springfield fought well on the whole. Their commanders, however, from Clinton and Knyphausen to Mathew and Wurmb (Simcoe being a notable exception), demonstrated half-heartedness bordering on the pathetic. The officers' refusal to press forward in the face of even mild adversity spoke volumes: they had no confidence in victory. The contrast on the other side of the lines could not have been greater. Distracted though they were by worry, internal squabbling, and even (in Maxwell's case) possibly liquor, Washington and his officers, except maybe Shreve, displayed confidence and courage on the battlefield.

Connecticut Farms and Springfield were significant for what they revealed, therefore, rather than for anything they decided. On paper, the military balance of power in the mid-Atlantic remained unchanged. Even Rochambeau's arrival accomplished nothing in the short term. These small battles nevertheless marked a palpable turning point in the Revolutionary War. Although Washington often has been unjustly accused of inactivity and indecision in the period between Monmouth and Yorktown, it was in fact Clinton's army that went dormant. In the aftermath of June 1780, that dormancy took a strong turn toward defeatism. The tide had definitely turned.

Notes

INTRODUCTION

1. Mark Lender, "The Politics of Battle: Washington, the Army, and the Monmouth Campaign," in *A Companion to George Washington*, ed. Edward G. Lengel (Malden, MA: Wiley-Blackwell, 2012), 226-244.

2. For a further development of this thesis, see Edward G. Lengel, *First Entrepreneur: How George Washington Built His—and the Nation's—Prosperity* (New York: Da Capo Press, 2016), 89-142.

3. Edward G. Lengel, "Assessing War: The Revolutionary War," in *Assessing War: The Challenge of Measuring Success and Failure,* ed. Leo Blanken, Jason Lepore, and Hy Rothstein (Washington, DC: Georgetown University Press, 2015), 65-80.

4. Andrew O'Shaughnessy, *The Men Who Lost America: British Leadership, the American Revolution, and the Fate of the Empire* (New Haven, CT: Yale University Press, 2013), 207-233.

5. Ibid., 230.

CHAPTER ONE: ARMAGEDDON IN VIEW

1. Thomas Fleming, *The Forgotten Victory: The Battle for New Jersey—1780* (New York: Reader's Digest Press, 1973), 37-38. Knyphausen lacks a good book-length biography in English, but see his entry in Mount Vernon's digital encyclopedia, https://www.mountvernon.org/library/digitalhistory/digital-encyclopedia/article/wilhelm-von-knyphausen/.

2. K.G. Davies, ed., *Documents of the American Revolution*, 1770–1783, 20 vols. (Shannon: Irish University Press, 1972-1981), 18:95-97.

3. For more on these officer resignations, see Edward G. Lengel et al., eds., *The Papers of George Washington: Revolutionary War Series,* 25 vols. (Charlottesville: University of Virginia Press, 1980-2016), 25:233-243.

4. Benjamin Huggins and Adrina Garbooshian-Huggins, eds., *The Papers of George Washington: Revolutionary War Series,* vol. 26 (Charlottesville: University of Virginia Press, 2019), 21-22, 186-88 (hereafter *PGW*).

5. *PGW*, 107, 216, 249-250.

6. *PGW*, 112, 114-118, 135-137, 168-171.

7. *PGW*, 194-196, 202-206; Joseph Plumb Martin, *Private Yankee Doodle: Being a Narrative of Some of the Adventures, Dangers and Sufferings of a Revolutionary Soldier,* ed. George F. Scheer (Boston: Little, Brown, 1962), 182-187.

8. *PGW*, 220-225.

9. *PGW*, 38-43, 258-260.

10. *PGW*, 166-172.

11. Lengel et al., eds., *Papers of George Washington,* 23:601-602.

12. Lengel et al., eds., *Papers of George Washington,* 25:433; *PGW*, 10-12; Robert K. Wright, *The Continental Army* (Washington, DC: US Army Center of Military History, 1983), 146-147.

13. Harry M. Ward, *General William Maxwell and the New Jersey Continentals* (Westport, CT: Greenwood Press, 1997), 73-74; Thomas Thorleifur Sobol, "William Maxwell, New Jersey's Hard Fighting General," *Journal of the American Revolution,* August 15, 2016, https://allthingsliberty.com/2016/08/william-maxwell-new-jerseys-hard-fighting-general/. See also Gabriel Neville, "The 'B' Team of 1777: Maxwell's Light Infantry," *Journal of the American Revolution,* April 10, 2018, https://allthingsliberty.com/2018/04/the-b-team-of-1777-maxwells-light-infantry/.

14. John U. Rees, "'One of the Best in the Army': An Overview of the New Jersey Brigade, 1775–1783," *Continental Soldier* 11, no. 2 (Spring 1998): 45-53.

15. The *Washington Papers* project generously refers to Alexander as "Stirling" in deference to his extremely tenuous claims to a Scottish earldom, but he will be referred to in this narrative as "Alexander" in order to avoid confusion with British brigadier general Thomas Stirling. Fleming has a poor opinion of the state of the New Jersey Brigade, dubbing the men "ragged [and] sullen," but as events proved, they were more solid than they seemed. Fleming, *Forgotten Victory,* 89-90.

16. *PGW*, 32-33, 93.

17. *PGW*, 68-70, 87-88.

18. *PGW*, 77-78, 95-96.

19. *PGW*, 155, 191-193.

20. *PGW*, 191-193; *New York Royal Gazette,* May 27; *New Jersey Gazette,* June 7; Fleming, *Forgotten Victory,* 87. Knox, who as a lieutenant with the 9th Pennsylvania Regiment in the reformed light infantry had been praised by Congress for lead-

ing the forlorn hope at Stony Point in July 1779, survived his awful wound, resigned his commission, and returned to his farm at Newark. He remained a committed patriot, however, and carried out some intelligence work for Washington in late summer 1781. "Beckwith, George, Sir (1753–1823) [British spy report]," 5 September 1781, GLC05224.01, Gilder Lehrman Collection, https://www.gilderlehrman.org/collection/glc0522401.

21. *PGW*, 211-212, 217-220, 237-239, 261.

22. *PGW*, 250-251, 261, 281, 288-292, 325-328, 330-331.

23. Fleming, *Forgotten Victory*, 28-36.

24. Fleming, 45-49; William Smith, *Historical Memoirs of William Smith*, ed. W.H.W. Sabine (New York: New York Times, 1971), 270.

25. Davies, *Documents*, 18:108, 110-111; Henry Clinton, *The American Rebellion: Sir Henry Clinton's Narrative of His Campaigns, 1775–1782, with an Appendix of Original Documents*, ed. William B. Willcox (New Haven, CT: Yale University Press, 1954), 192-93.

26. This arrangement somewhat contradicts those provided by Fleming and Carl Leopold Baurmeister, *Revolution in America: Confidential Letters and Journals, 1776–1784, of Adjutant General Major Baurmeister of the Hessian Forces*, trans. and ann. Bernhard A. Uhlendorf (New Brunswick, NJ: Rutgers University Press, 1957), 352-53. It derives from Knyphausen's after-action report: Knyphausen report to Landgraf Friedrich II of Hessen Cassel, July 2, 1780, Letter GG (Part 1), Correspondence of General Knyphausen, Oct. 1779–1780, pp. 188-199, Lidgerwood Collection, Morristown National Park, microfiche accessed at David Library of the American Revolution, Washington Crossing, PA (hereafter Knyphausen report). See also Bruce E. Burgoyne, trans., *Journal kept by the Distinguished Hessian Field Jaeger Corps during the Campaigns of the Royal Army of Great Britain in North America* (privately printed, 1986), 188.

27. Knyphausen report; Davies, *Documents*, 18:108, 110-111. Fleming erroneously has both Mathew's and Tryon's divisions sailing in schooners from Manhattan. Knyphausen's report makes clear, however, that Mathew's division was already stationed on Manhattan. I have assumed, although Knyphausen is not clear on this point, that the intention was for Stirling and Tryon to land at Elizabethtown Point and for the latter to push forward with the Jäger Corps in advance and Knyphausen in close command, while the flat-bottomed boats returned to bring Mathew's troops across. The weather and logistical difficulties on Staten Island significantly disrupted these plans. Instead of advancing in the order Tryon, Stirling, Mathew, then, the attackers advanced in the order Stirling, Mathew, Tryon.

CHAPTER 2: THE BATTLE OF CONNECTICUT FARMS, JUNE 7, 1780

1. Fleming, *Forgotten Victory*, 117-120; Clinton, *American Rebellion*, 191; Baurmeister, *Revolution*, 352; Knyphausen report.

2. Knyphausen report; Fleming, *Forgotten Victory*, 114-117.

3. Stirling quote from Colin Calloway, *The Scratch of a Pen: 1763 and the Transformation of North America* (New York: Oxford University Press, 2006), 83.

4. *PGW*, 347.

5. Rodney Atwood, *The Hessians: Mercenaries from Hessen-Kassel in the American Revolution* (New York: Cambridge University Press, 1980), 43-44. The British surgeon initially wanted to amputate Stirling's leg, but he refused. He survived his wound despite a long, painful recovery and died in 1808 (James Home to William Home, 28 June 1780, Gilder Lehrman Collection; *Oxford Dictionary of National Biography*). *PGW* and Fleming erroneously claim that Stirling's successor was Lieutenant Colonel Ludwig Adolph von Wurmb, who commanded the Jäger Corps. As previously indicated, however, that unit marched with Tryon's rather than Stirling's division (Fleming, *Forgotten Victory*, 98; *PGW*, 341; see also Knyphausen report). Thanks to Eric Schnitzer, historian at Saratoga National Historical Park, for helping to sort out the confusion between the two Wurmbs.

6. *PGW*, 349; Charles A. Lesser, ed., *Sinews of Independence: Monthly Strength Reports of the Continental Army* (Chicago: University of Chicago Press, 1976), 168.

7. *PGW*, 349-351.

8. Fleming, *Forgotten Victory*, 123-126; see also note 5 to this chapter. Various versions of the encounter appeared in newspapers at the time and were lavishly embellished in years to come.

9. Edwin F. Hatfield, *History of Elizabeth, New Jersey: Including the Early History of Union County* (New York: Carlton & Lanahan, 1868), 488-489; Davies, *Documents*, 18:110; *Documents Relating to the Revolutionary History of the State of New Jersey*, ser. 2, vol. 4, ed. William Nelson (Trenton: State Gazette Publishing, 1914), 414 (hereafter *DRRHSNJ*); see also *Historical Magazine* 8, 2nd ser. (July 1870): 55-56. Fleming provides far more detailed versions of these encounters, but his sources for dialogue and description are unclear. His accounts include a detailed description of the death of young Jonathan Crane, son of Mayor Stephen Crane, who is supposed to have died of "shock and grief" after his son ended his life spitted on a Hessian bayonet. However, the Crane family genealogy Fleming cites as his source indicates only that Jonathan was "killed by the Hessian soldiers" sometime in June 1780, and that Stephen died on June 23; Hatfield does not mention either death. Fleming, *Forgotten Victory*, 127-128, 136-139; Ellery Bicknell Crane, *Genealogy of the Crane Family* (Worcester, MA: Charles Hamilton, 1900), 2:473.

10. W. Woodford Clayton, *History of Union and Middlesex Counties, New Jersey, with Biographical Sketches of Many of Their Prominent Men* (Philadelphia: Everts & Peck, 1882), 178-79, 376, 381.

11. William Maxwell to William Livingston, June 14, Livingston Papers, New York Public Library; Aaron Ogden, *Autobiography of Col. Aaron Ogden, of Elizabethtown* (Paterson, NJ: The Press, 1893), 12-13. In his memoirs, Ogden, who claims to have twice saved Maxwell from "ruin and defeat," suggests that the decision

to pull back from Jelf's Hill was made on the spot between himself and Dayton with no instructions from Maxwell. If so, Maxwell was guilty of shocking neglect; but it is more likely that this experienced and competent general had planned for these circumstances and instructed Dayton, through Ogden, to do as he did.

12. Maxwell to Livingston, June 14, Livingston Papers. By "the roads leading to the right and left," Maxwell clearly was referring to the Vauxhall Road on his left and probably to smaller tracks and pathways to his right, either of which could have been used to outflank him. Hessian jäger officer Johann Ewald remarked, in a description quoted by *PGW* and reflected in its map of the encounter, that Maxwell's "front was covered by a marshy brook which cut through a range of hills and by marshy woodlands. . . . [O]ne could not get near this position at all, because of the narrow approaches at the flanks which the Americans had strongly occupied." Ewald was not present, however, and his description likely refers not to the "steep defile" that Dayton defended here and again on June 23 (when Colonel John Graves Simcoe overcame it without difficulty), but to a position that Maxwell occupied—but did not defend—with his main forces further back. Alternately, Ewald may just have been misinformed. Johann Ewald, *Diary of the American War: A Hessian Journal*, trans. and ed. Joseph P. Tustin (New Haven, CT: Yale University Press, 1979), 244; Burgoyne, *Journal*, 188.

13. Smith's exceptionally important letter to Washington of Nov. 10, 1780, was (strangely) overlooked by the editors of *PGW* and Fleming, despite its existence in the *Washington Papers* at the Library of Congress, and in the Founders Online edition of the *Washington Papers*. Though self-justifying and written in response to a later controversy with Colonel Israel Shreve of the 2nd New Jersey Regiment, the letter provides extensive and vital first-hand testimony of the Battles of Connecticut Farms and Springfield. In it, Smith indicates that while he and Dayton commanded at the defile, the better part of Smith's merged command of the 1st and Spencer's regiments remained with Maxwell, until Smith rejoined the main body after the defile was abandoned. See also *PGW*, 218-220, 429-430.

14. Maxwell to Livingston, June 14, Livingston Papers.

15. Maxwell to Livingston, June 14, Livingston Papers; Burgoyne, *Journal*, 188-189; Fleming, *Forgotten Victory*, 152-155; Knyphausen report.

16. *DRRHSNJ*, 415-418, 421-424, 445-446.

17. *DRRHSNJ*, 415-418, 421-424, 445-446. For an investigation of this affair, see John Smith Jr., "Hannah Caldwell's Death: Accident or Murder," *Journal of the American Revolution*, August 4, 2015, https://allthingsliberty.com/2015/08/hannah-caldwells-death-accident-or-murder/#_edn1.

18. For example, *New-Jersey Gazette* (Trenton), June 21, 1780, and *New-Jersey Journal* (Chatham), June 21, 1780. For British accounts, see *New York Royal Gazette*, no. 389, June 21, 1780, and *New York Royal Gazette*, No. 402, August 5, 1780. On balance, the British accounts seem more compelling, and Fleming's *Forgotten Victory*, 77, believes as much. But there is no conclusive evidence either way.

19. Burgoyne, *Journal,* 189; George Mathew, "Mathew's Narrative," ed. Thomas Balch, *Historical Magazine* 1 (April 1857): 104.

20. Maxwell to Livingston, June 14, Livingston Papers; Smith to Washington, Nov. 10, 1780, Library of Congress; Knyphausen report. Fleming misplaces this encounter in the center of Connecticut Farms, before the action had even reached Caldwell's house. Fleming, *Forgotten Victory,* 159-163.

21. Knyphausen report; Burgoyne, *Journal,* 189-190.

22. Milton M. Klein and Ronald W. Howard, eds., *The Twilight of British Rule in Revolutionary America: The New York Letter Book of General James Robertson, 1780-1783* (Cooperstown, NY: New York State Historical Association, 1983), 128.

23. Knyphausen report; Klein and Howard, *Twilight,* 126.

24. *PGW,* 342-343; Burgoyne, *Journal,* 190.

25. *PGW,* 349; Smith to Washington, Nov. 10, 1780, Library of Congress; Joseph H. Jones, ed., *The Life of Ashbel Green* (New York: R. Carter & Brothers, 1849), 109.

26. Richard K. Showman et al., eds., *The Papers of General Nathanael Greene,* 13 vols. (Chapel Hill: University of North Carolina Press, 1976-2005), 13:597-598; Mathew, "Mathew's Narrative," 104-105; Fleming, *Forgotten Victory,* 169-170.

27. Stephen Conway, "To Subdue America: British Army Officers and the Conduct of the Revolutionary War," *William and Mary Quarterly,* 3rd ser., no. 43 (1986): 382, 392-399; Stephen Conway, *The War of American Independence, 1775–1783* (London: Edward Arnold, 1995), 35, 39, 51-52, 166.

28. Hatfield, *History,* 487ff.; Davies, *Documents,* 18:108; Smith, *Historical Memoirs,* 281; Burgoyne, *Journal,* 190.

29. Mathew, "Mathew's Narrative," 104-105.

30. *PGW,* 342-343, 351-352.

31. *PGW,* 354-355.

32. Quoted in *PGW,* 352; *DRRHSNJ,* 417, 445.

33. PGW, 344; John Hills, "Sketch of the Position of the British Forces at Elizabethtown Point after their Return from Connecticut Farm, in the Province of East Jersey: under the Command of His Excelly Leiutt Genl. Knyphausen, on the 8th June 1780," Library of Congress.

34. Jones, *Life of Ashbel Green,* 111-112.

35. *PGW,* 344; Hills, "Sketch"; Johann Carl Philipp von Krafft, *Journal of John Charles Philip von Krafft, Lieutenant in the Hessian Regiment von Bose 1776–1784,* ed. Thomas H. Edsall (New York: privately printed, 1888), 112-113; Jones, *Life of Ashbel Green,* 113; Knyphausen report; *Journal of the Regiment von Donop, 1776–84,* Lidgerwood Collection, Letter E (hereafter Donop Journal). *PGW* erroneously suggests in its inset map of the Battle of Connecticut Farms that Hand succeeded in pressing his attack right to the edge of Knyphausen's fortifications at Elizabethtown Point. In fact, the Americans came nowhere near the water's

edge. That, and other *PGW* errors, are corrected in the maps of the Battles of Connecticut Farms and Springfield appearing in this book. *PGW*, 348.

36. *PGW*, 353-354; Smith, *Historical Memoirs*, 272.

37. *PGW*, 344, 352-355.

38. Knyphausen report; Ewald, *Diary*, 245; Smith, *Historical Memoirs*, 273; Howard Henry Peckham, *The Toll of Independence: Engagements and Battle Casualties of the American Revolution* (Chicago: University of Chicago Press, 1974), 71; Maxwell to Livingston, June 14, Livingston Papers; *PGW*, 365, 419-420.

39. Maxwell to Livingston, June 14, Livingston Papers; *PGW*, 374-375, 392-394.

40. Maxwell to Livingston, June 14, Livingston Papers; Mathew, "Mathew's Narrative," 104-105; Davies, *Documents*, 18:110; Clinton, *American Rebellion*, 192; Archibald Robertson, *Archibald Robertson, Lieutenant General Royal Engineers: His Diaries and Sketches in America, 1762–1780*, ed. Harry Miller Lydenberg (New York: New York Public Library, 1930); 232; Smith, *Historical Memoirs*, 272-273.

CHAPTER 3: CLINTON ARRIVES

1. *PGW*, 357, 364-365, 374-375, 391-392, 437; James Thacher, *Military Journal of the American Revolution, from the Commencement to the Disbanding of the American Army: Comprising a Detailed Account of the Principal Events and Battles of the Revolution, with Their Exact Dates, and a Biographical Sketch of the Most Prominent Generals* (Hartford, CT: Hurlbut, Williams, 1862), 200; "Letters of General Henry Lee," *Virginia Magazine of History and Biography* 6, no. 2 (October 1898): 153-155.

2. *PGW*, 362, 364-365. See also Paul David Nelson, *The Life of William Alexander, Lord Stirling: George Washington's Noble General* (Tuscaloosa: University of Alabama Press, 1987), 156-157.

3. *PGW*, 367-368.

4. *PGW*, 383-384, 398, 412-414. Although the latter quotation appears in the camp committee circular, it reflects the commander in chief's opinions as expressed in consultation.

5. *PGW*, 374-375, 418-419.

6. *PGW*, 365, 369, 374-375, 383-384, 453; Paul H. Smith, et al., eds., *Letters of Delegates to Congress, 1774–1789*, 25 vols. (Washington, DC: Library of Congress, 1976–98), 15:297–298.

7. *PGW*, 412-414, 424-425, 429-430, 435. By nature an impatient man of action, and believing by conviction that time was not on America's side, Washington always suffered at times such as these. Revealingly, he wrote to the camp committee on June 12 that the lack of military resources would "infallibly compel us to confine ourselves to a mere defensive plan, except as to some little, partial indecisive enterprises against remote points; and will of course disappoint the expectations of our allies and protract the war." *PGW*, 397-399.

8. John Graves Simcoe, *Simcoe's Military Journal* (New York: Bartlett & Wellford, 1844), 143; Knyphausen report. Knyphausen's scouts told him the closest estab-

lished American outpost was at Liberty Hall. "It is nearly impossible to surprise the enemy at any time," the Jäger Corps journal grumbled after the June 13 encounter, "because every house one passes is, so to speak, an advance post, because the farmer or his son, also his wife and daughter, shoot a rocket up or run along the footpaths to report to the enemy." Burgoyne, *Journal*, 195.

9. *PGW*, 417-418, 428, 426, 428-429, 457-458; Knyphausen report; *Donop Journal*; Krafft, *Journal*, 114; Mathew, "Mathew's Narrative," 105.

10. *PGW*, 59, 440-443, 447-451.

11. Mathew, "Mathew's Narrative," 105; Knyphausen report.

12. *PGW*, 364, 449-451, 455-459, 463-464, 474, 489-490; Knyphausen report; Robertson, *Archibald Robertson*, 232; Krafft, *Journal*, 114.

13. *PGW*, 469-470, 492, 496, 498-499, 503, 513-514. On June 20, Lee developed plans for a determined two-pronged assault on Knyphausen's positions at Elizabethtown Point, but whether he presented that plan to Greene is unknown, and in any case it never came off. "Letters of General Henry Lee," 153-155.

14. Clinton, *American Rebellion*, 190-191.

15. Smith, *Historical Memoirs*, 282-286; Robertson, *Archibald Robertson*, 230-32; Clinton, *American Rebellion*, 192-193. "The enemy are worse off than we are," General William Irvine wrote to his wife from camp in the Short Hills on June 18. "They have no tents and are hemmed in a narrow neck of land, whilst we have a wide extent of country." Hatfield, *History*, 496.

16. Clinton, *American Rebellion*, 190-193; Robertson, *Archibald Robertson*, 233; Davies, *Documents*, 18:112-114; Carl Van Doren, *Secret History of the American Revolution: An Account of the Conspiracies of Benedict Arnold and Numerous Others, Drawn from the Secret Service Papers of the British Headquarters in North America, Now for the First Time Examined and Made Public* (Garden City, NY: Garden City Publishing, 1941), 460.

17. *PGW*, 504-505, 507-508; Knyphausen report; Simcoe, *Military Journal*, 143.

CHAPTER 4: THE BATTLE OF SPRINGFIELD, JUNE 23, 1780

1. Knyphausen report. Fleming places the 42nd Regiment of Foot with the 2nd Division. *Forgotten Victory*, 232-233. But Knyphausen does not mention it in his report. It probably marched with Clinton.

2. Fleming imagines a dramatic planning conference between Knyphausen and a grimly smiling Clinton, in which the two generals, their fingers roving smoothly over a map, plotted their attack. *Forgotten Victory*, 232-233. No evidence for such a conference exists, and whether Knyphausen devised or was directed to carry out this two-pronged attack remains unclear. The assault does, however, seem to have been plotted more aggressively than Clinton's intentions warranted.

3. Clayton, *Union and Middlesex Counties*, 179, 366.

4. Knyphausen report; *PGW*, 520, 522, 529-532; Smith to Washington, Nov. 10, 1780, Library of Congress.

5. Simcoe, *Military Journal*, 143-144. Fleming, drawing on a letter of July 15, 1780, from Lieutenant Colonel Benoni Hathaway of the New Jersey militia to Governor Livingston, accusing Brigadier General Nathaniel Heard of a disorderly retreat "sum Time in June last 1780," characterizes Dayton's retreat in the same manner. *Forgotten Victory*, 324-325. On closer inspection, however, it is impossible to identify certainly where, or even when, the episode described by the semiliterate Hathaway took place. Andrew W. Sherman, *Historic Morristown, New Jersey: The Story of Its First Century* (Morristown, NJ: Howard Publishing, 1905), 368-370.

6. Knyphausen report; *PGW*, 522, 529-532.

7. There is considerable confusion over Lee's dispositions, and indeed Greene himself was unclear on what actually took place on his left flank. Sadly, anything that Lee may have written about the encounter is no longer extant. Contemporary accounts—especially Simcoe's *Military Journal*—suggest that Lee placed outposts at Vauxhall Bridge over the east branch of the Rahway, just west of Vauxhall at what is now the intersection of Millburn Avenue and Vauxhall Road, while he conducted his main defense a mile to the west at Little's Bridge, which seems to have been at or near what is now Egbeson's Bridge over the west branch of the Rahway, near the intersection of what is now Millburn Avenue and Main Street. Many subsequent accounts, however, either conflate the two bridges or suggest that Lee's main defensive stand took place at the eastern rather than the western bridge (see, for example, Ward, *General William Maxwell*, 155; the *Item of Millburn and Short Hills*, Sept. 28, 1961). The Vauxhall Bridge, in fact, has long been the one marked by a state battle plaque.

Fleming reinforced this perception by describing a major encounter at the Vauxhall Bridge, where "muskets boomed and ex-neighbors spilled each other's blood with appalling ferocity." *Forgotten Victory*, 269. Simcoe, however, makes clear that he encountered no opposition at the first bridge he crossed at about 9:00 AM (when he heard the cannonading begin between Angell's field piece and Knyphausen's artillery). This must have been the Vauxhall Bridge. Both Simcoe and Greene describe how the contested bridge crossing—which took place at 11:00 AM, when Knyphausen heard loud fire off to his right—was followed immediately by the Loyalists taking possession of high ground, an action that forced Lee to "give up the pass." This would only make sense if it took place on a bridge over the west bank of the Rahway (the terrain behind the Vauxhall Bridge is flat and passless until Millburn Avenue approaches the western bridge south of Newark Mountain, below Washington Rock).

Nor would a strong defense of the advanced and exposed Vauxhall Bridge have made tactical sense for Lee, whose prime objective was to defend the road through the Short Hills to Hobart Gap and who would have wanted to remain in supporting distance of the troops in and behind Springfield. Finally, contem-

porary British accounts and Knyphausen's report describe Simcoe's and
Mathew's troops filing off to the left after the contested bridge crossing and
moving cross-country or by small paths along the Rahway toward Knyphausen's
force in Springfield late in the morning of June 23—a move that would only
have been possible from the bridge over the west bank of the Rahway.

8. *PGW*, 529-532; Showman, *Green Papers*, 6:39; Knyphausen report.

9. *PGW*, 525-526, 529-532. Fleming elaborates this movement with a somewhat
confusing account of a dispute over the conduct of Lieutenant Colonel Cosmo
Gordon, which subsequently led to his court-martial. *Forgotten Victory*, 269, 283-
285.

10. Jeremiah Greenman, *Diary of a Common Soldier in the American Revolution,
1775–1783: An Annotated Edition of the Military Journal of Jeremiah Greenman*, ed.
Robert C. Bray and Paul E. Bushnell (DeKalb: Northern Illinois University Press,
1978), 174-175; the Jäger Corps journal attributes the attack to the 38th Regiment of Foot, but the casualty figures do not support this. Burgoyne, *Journal*,
199. Knyphausen, who of course ordered the attack, reported that it began
about 11:00 AM. Letters from Greene and Major David Humphreys written at
the same time, however, describe Springfield as captured and the engagement
essentially over—either somebody was wrong about the timing, or the struggle
for the bridge and Springfield took far less time than is generally assumed.
Knyphausen report; Fleming, *Forgotten Victory*, 269; *PGW*, 523-524, 528-532.

11. Clayton, *Union and Middlesex Counties*, 370.

12. Burgoyne, *Journal*, 199-200.

13. Greenman, *Diary*, 174-175; Jones, *Life of Ashbel Green*, 117-118; Thacher, *Military Journal*, 240-241; C.R. Williams, ed., *Revolutionary Heroes: Containing the Life
of Brigadier Gen. William Barton, and Also, of Captain Stephen Olney* (Providence,
RI: privately published, 1839), 253; Washington Irving, *Life of Washington*, 5 vols.
(New York: G.P. Putnam, 1856), 4:95; *PGW*, 528-532. Greene's tally of casualties
at the end of the battle indicated that the artillery had lost three killed and two
wounded—probably all from the crew of this lone gun. Ashbel Green reported
that the British infantry "broke and rallied three times" before the jägers forded
the Rahway, inspiring a fanciful depiction of the battle by Fleming, *Forgotten Victory*. Green admittedly was not an eyewitness, however, and so I have followed
Greenman's more plausible account.

14. This may have been the moment when, sometime around 11:00 AM and only
shortly after Knyphausen began his attack, Greene and Humphreys decided that
Springfield was already lost, though fighting continued to take place there.
PGW, 523-524, 528-529.

15. Greene's tally of casualties at the end of the battle indicated that Angell's
regiment had suffered more heavily than any other, with six killed, thirty-two
wounded, and three missing. *PGW*, 531-532.

16. Fleming, describes this affair with typically fanciful detail, claiming that "well over two dozen . . . redcoats" fell here and about an equal number of militia and continentals. *Forgotten Victory*, 265. However, Fleming bases his account on a nebulous reference by Greene to a brief and inconclusive attack by Brigadier General Philemon Dickinson's militia that might have happened at any other place or time. And the fact that Shreve's and Spencer's regiments suffered a mere handful of casualties over the course of the entire battle—and that the American militia as a whole suffered none killed and about a dozen wounded over the course of the battle—suggests that the second bridge defense did not last long and that the affair of the stone house was equally brief if it happened at all. *PGW*, 529-532. Neither Greene nor Smith say anything about the stone house, and Knyphausen's report is sadly unilluminating on the whole struggle for Springfield.

17. Francis B. Heitman, comp., *Historical Register of Officers of the Continental Army during the War of the Revolution, April 1775 to December 1783* (Washington, DC: Rare Book Shop Publishing, 1914), 495; Fleming, *Forgotten Victory*, 235-266; William Y. Thompson, *Israel Shreve: Revolutionary War Officer* (Ruston, LA: McGinty Trust Fund Publications, 1979); John Shreve, "A Short Account of My Life [1853]," in L. P. Allen, *The Genealogy and History of the Shreve Family from 1641* (Greenfield, IL: privately printed, 1901), 348.

18. Smith to Washington, Nov. 10, 1780, Library of Congress; *PGW*, 523-524. This letter originated in a later dispute among the regimental commanders of the New Jersey Brigade. Other correspondence pertaining to the dispute has apparently been lost. Smith, not the most ethical of officers, may have exaggerated Shreve's cowardly conduct, but there also is circumstantial evidence to suggest Washington was eager to get the corpulent colonel out of the army. For his part, the frequently impecunious Shreve was engaged that summer in a fairly desperate correspondence about his miserable finances with his wife, who also was eager to get him back home. Israel Shreve to Mary Shreve, July 27, 1780, Shreve Papers, University of Houston. https://digital.lib.uh.edu/collection/p15195coll12/item/152.

19. *PGW*, 523-524, 528-532.

20. *PGW*, 513-514, 522-534; Clinton, *American Rebellion*, 194; Showman, *Green Papers*, 6:40.

21. Klein and Howard, *Twilight*, 126.

22. The Jäger Corps journal describes how the troops "composed the rear guard and could hardly make their way between the fires of the already collapsing houses." Burgoyne, *Journal*, 200.

23. Mathew, "Mathew's Narrative," 105; Clinton, *American Rebellion*, 194; *DR-RHSNJ*, 464; *PGW*, 523-524, 527-532.

24. Knyphausen report; Peckham, *Toll of Independence*, 71; Robertson, *Archibald Robertson*, 233; Clinton, *American Rebellion*, 194; Fleming, *Forgotten Victory*, 286;

Ewald, *Diary*, 245-246; Thacher, *Military Journal*, 201.

25. *PGW*, 529-532; Showman, *Green Papers*, 6:39; *DRRHSNJ*, 475.

CONCLUSION

1.*PGW*, 557, 563.

2.O'Shaughnessy, *The Men Who Lost America*, 233-234.

Bibliography

Atwood, Rodney. *The Hessians: Mercenaries from Hessen-Kassel in the American Revolution.* New York: Cambridge University Press, 1980.

Barber, John Warner, and Henry Howe. *Historical Collections of the State of New Jersey.* New York: S. Tuttle, 1844.

Baurmeister, Carl Leopold. *Revolution in America: Confidential Letters and Journals, 1776–1784, of Adjutant General Major Baurmeister of the Hessian Forces.* Translated and annotated by Bernhard A. Uhlendorf. New Brunswick, NJ: Rutgers University Press, 1957.

Burgoyne, Bruce E., trans. *Journal kept by the Distinguished Hessian Field Jaeger Corps during the Campaigns of the Royal Army of Great Britain in North America.* Privately printed, 1986.

Calloway, Colin. *The Scratch of a Pen: 1763 and the Transformation of North America.* New York: Oxford University Press, 2006.

Clayton, W. Woodford. *History of Union and Middlesex Counties, New Jersey, with Biographical Sketches of Many of Their Prominent Men.* Philadelphia: Everts & Peck, 1882.

Clinton, Henry. *The American Rebellion: Sir Henry Clinton's Narrative of His Campaigns, 1775–1782, with an Appendix of Original Documents.* Edited by William B. Willcox. New Haven, CT: Yale University Press, 1954.

Conway, Stephen. "To Subdue America: British Army Officers and the Conduct of the Revolutionary War." *William and Mary Quarterly*, 3rd ser., no. 43 (1986): 381-407.

———. *The War of American Independence, 1775–1783*. London: Edward Arnold, 1995.

Crane, Ellery Bicknell. *Genealogy of the Crane Family*. Worcester, MA: Charles Hamilton, 1900.

Davies, K.G., ed. *Documents of the American Revolution, 1770–1783*. 20 vols. Shannon: Irish University Press, 1972–1981.

Documents Relating to the Revolutionary History of the State of New Jersey. Series 2, vol. 4. Edited by William Nelson. Trenton: State Gazette Publishing, 1914.

Ewald, Johann. *Diary of the American War: A Hessian Journal*. Translated and edited by Joseph P. Tustin. New Haven, CT: Yale University Press, 1979.

Fleming, Thomas. *The Forgotten Victory: The Battle for New Jersey—1780*. New York: Reader's Digest Press, 1973.

———. *The Strategy of Victory: How General George Washington Won the American Revolution*. New York: Da Capo Press, 2017.

Greenman, Jeremiah. *Diary of a Common Soldier in the American Revolution, 1775–1783: An Annotated Edition of the Military Journal of Jeremiah Greenman*. Edited by Robert C. Bray and Paul E. Bushnell. DeKalb: Northern Illinois University Press, 1978.

Hatfield, Edwin F. *History of Elizabeth, New Jersey: Including the Early History of Union County*. New York: Carlton & Lanahan, 1868.

Heitman, Francis B., comp. *Historical Register of Officers of the Continental Army during the War of the Revolution, April 1775 to December 1783*. Washington, DC: Rare Book Shop Publishing, 1914.

Hills, John. "Sketch of the Position of the British Forces at Elizabethtown Point after their Return from Connecticut Farm, in the Province of East Jersey: under the Command of His Excelly Leiutt Genl. Knyphausen, on the 8th June 1780." Library of Congress.

Huggins, Benjamin, and Adrina Garbooshian-Huggins, eds. *The Papers of George Washington: Revolutionary War Series*. Vol. 26. Charlottesville: University of Virginia Press, 2019.

Irving, Washington. *Life of George Washington.* Hudson Edition. 5 vols. New York: G.P. Putnam's Sons, 1887.

Jones, Joseph H., ed. *The Life of Ashbel Green.* New York: R. Carter & Brothers, 1849.

Klein, Milton M., and Ronald W. Howard, eds. *The Twilight of British Rule in Revolutionary America: The New York Letter Book of General James Robertson, 1780–1783.* Cooperstown, NY: New York State Historical Association, 1983.

Knyphausen, Wilhelm von. Report to Landgraf Friedrich II of Hessen Cassel, July 2, 1780, Letter GG (Part 1), Correspondence of General Knyphausen, Oct. 1779–1780, pp. 188-199, Lidgerwood Collection, Morristown National Park, microfilm accessed at David Library of the American Revolution, Washington Crossing, PA.

Krafft, Johann Carl Philipp von. *Journal of John Charles Philip von Krafft, Lieutenant in the Hessian Regiment von Bose 1776–1784.* Edited by Thomas H. Edsall. New York: privately printed, 1888.

Lender, Mark. "The Politics of Battle: Washington, the Army, and the Monmouth Campaign." In *A Companion to George Washington,* edited by Edward G. Lengel. Malden, MA: Wiley-Blackwell, 2012, 226–244.

Lengel, Edward G. "Assessing War: The Revolutionary War." In *Assessing War: The Challenge of Measuring Success and Failure,* edited by Leo Blanken, Jason Lepore, and Hy Rothstein. Washington, DC: Georgetown University Press, 2015, 65–80.

———. *First Entrepreneur: How George Washington Built His—and the Nation's—Prosperity.* New York: Da Capo Press, 2016.

Lengel, Edward G., et al., eds., *The Papers of George Washington: Revolutionary War Series.* 25 vols. Charlottesville: University of Virginia Press, 1980–2016.

Lesser, Charles A., ed. *Sinews of Independence: Monthly Strength Reports of the Continental Army.* Chicago: University of Chicago Press, 1976.

"Letters of General Henry Lee." *Virginia Magazine of History and Biography* 6, no. 2 (October 1898): 153–155.

Martin, Joseph Plumb. *Private Yankee Doodle: Being a Narrative of Some of the Adventures, Dangers and Sufferings of a Revolutionary Soldier.* Edited by George F. Scheer. Boston: Little, Brown, 1962.

Mathew, George. "Mathew's Narrative." Edited by Thomas Balch. *Historical Magazine* 1 (April 1857): 102–106.

Nelson, Paul David. *The Life of William Alexander, Lord Stirling: George Washington's Noble General.* Tuscaloosa: University of Alabama Press, 1987.

Neville, Gabriel. "The 'B' Team of 1777: Maxwell's Light Infantry." *Journal of the American Revolution*, April 10, 2018. https://allthings liberty.com/2018/04/the-b-team-of-1777-maxwells-light-infantry/.

Ogden, Aaron. *Autobiography of Col. Aaron Ogden, of Elizabethtown.* Paterson, NJ: The Press, 1893.

O'Shaughnessy, Andrew. *The Men Who Lost America: British Leadership, the American Revolution, and the Fate of the Empire.* New Haven, CT: Yale University Press, 2013.

Peckham, Howard Henry. *The Toll of Independence: Engagements and Battle Casualties of the American Revolution.* Chicago: University of Chicago Press, 1974.

Rees, John U. "'One of the Best in the Army': An Overview of the New Jersey Brigade, 1775–1783." *Continental Soldier* 11, no. 2 (Spring 1998): 45–53.

Robertson, Archibald. *Archibald Robertson, Lieutenant General Royal Engineers: His Diaries and Sketches in America, 1762–1780.* Edited by Harry Miller Lydenberg. New York: New York Public Library, 1930.

Sherman, Andrew W. *Historic Morristown, New Jersey: The Story of Its First Century.* Morristown, NJ: Howard Publishing, 1905.

Showman, Richard K., et al., eds. *The Papers of General Nathanael Greene.* 13 vols. Chapel Hill: University of North Carolina Press, 1976–2005.

Shreve, John. "A Short Account of My Life [1853]." In L. P. Allen, *The Genealogy and History of the Shreve Family from 1641.* Greenfield, IL: privately printed, 1901.

Simcoe, John Graves. *Simcoe's Military Journal.* New York: Bartlett & Wellford, 1844.

Smith, John, Jr., "Hannah Caldwell's Death: Accident or Murder." *Journal of the American Revolution*, August 4, 2015. https://allth-ingsliberty.com/2015/08/hannah-caldwells-death-accident-or-murder/#_edn1.

Smith, Paul H., et al., eds. *Letters of Delegates to Congress, 1774–1789.* 25 vols. Washington, DC: Library of Congress, 1976–98.

Smith, William. *Historical Memoirs of William Smith.* Edited by W.H.W. Sabine. New York: New York Times, 1971.

Sobol, Thomas Thorleifur. "William Maxwell, New Jersey's Hard Fighting General." *Journal of the American Revolution,* August 15, 2016. https://allthingsliberty.com/2016/08/william-maxwell-new-jerseys-hard-fighting-general/.

Thacher, James. *Military Journal of the American Revolution, from the Commencement to the Disbanding of the American Army: Comprising a Detailed Account of the Principal Events and Battles of the Revolution, with Their Exact Dates, and a Biographical Sketch of the Most Prominent Generals.* Hartford, CT: Hurlbut, Williams, 1862.

Thompson, William Y. *Israel Shreve: Revolutionary War Officer.* Ruston, LA: McGinty Trust Fund Publications, 1979.

Van Doren, Carl. *Secret History of the American Revolution: An Account of the Conspiracies of Benedict Arnold and Numerous Others, Drawn from the Secret Service Papers of the British Headquarters in North America, Now for the First Time Examined and Made Public.* Garden City, NY: Garden City Publishing, 1941.

Ward, Harry M. *General William Maxwell and the New Jersey Continentals.* Westport, CT: Greenwood Press, 1997.

Williams, C.R., ed. *Revolutionary Heroes: Containing the Life of Brigadier Gen. William Barton, and Also, of Captain Stephen Olney.* Providence, RI: privately published, 1839.

Wright, Robert K. *The Continental Army.* Washington, DC: US Army Center of Military History, 1983.

Acknowledgments

ONE THING I HAVE LEARNED over the course of my professional career is the difference between sitting in a corner editing and going out and talking to people. After nearly twenty years' dedicated service to the *Washington Papers*, I recognize the lure of collections of historical documents. To those who work on them every day to the exclusion of all else, Washington's letters eventually may seem not just to reveal but to embody truth. Whatever isn't there, it can seem, either doesn't exist or isn't worth knowing. All too many academic administrators reinforce this blinkered mindset by defining those who work on historical manuscripts as editors rather than historians. The real tragedy takes place when editors embrace that definition instead of working to transcend it, becoming latter-day Bartleby the scriveners. Fear, as always, is the great enemy.

This book benefits tremendously from the input of professionals who discussed it with me and directed me to readily available and vital sources I might have overlooked had I been working in a more cloistered editorial environment. First among them is Donald M. Londahl-Smidt. After I presented a preliminary draft of my thesis at the superb American Revolutionary War Round Table of Bergen County, New Jersey, Don strongly advised me to

take a look at Lieutenant General Wilhelm von Knyphausen's reports on these battles, along with other German documents in
the Lidgerwood Collection held on microfiche at the David Library of the American Revolution. He then contacted Kathie Ludwig, librarian at the David Library, who provided me with files of
the relevant documents and then facilitated, along with Meg Mc-
Sweeney, my research trip in August 2019.

As this book demonstrates, Knyphausen's report and other
German accounts—long available but mostly ignored—put an entirely new complexion on the battle narratives presented in previous, even recent, books and edited volumes. Even so, it took my
research only so far. Eric Schnitzer, park ranger and historian at
Saratoga National Historical Park, helped in particular to solve a
puzzle that had baffled me regarding the true identity of the
"Wurmb" who commanded Knyphausen's first division during
most of the Battle of Connecticut Farms. My friend Rick Britton,
the always-brilliant historical cartographer, incorporated this and
other discoveries in the redrawn maps that appear in this book.

My friend Bruce Venter deserves thanks more than anyone
for his creation of the Conference on the American Revolution
that takes place annually during the third weekend of March in
Williamsburg, Virginia. This conference, subsequently emulated
by Brian Mack and Norm Bollen's annual Revolutionary War conference in Fort Plain, New York, demonstrates more than anything else what happens when people from different
backgrounds, including professionals and amateurs, cross bound-
aries and share knowledge. Nowhere have I learned more about
this period of history, or enjoyed myself more in a professional
setting, than at these conferences.

It's probably not a stretch to say that these conferences in-
spired—or at least hosted—the creation of this new series for
Westholme Publishing. Bruce H. Franklin, now also running the
fertile *Journal of the American Revolution,* has been a force at the
Williamsburg conference since its conception. In addition to pur-
veying his many excellent book titles, Bruce always enjoys dis-
cussing new research and fresh book ideas. When Mark Lender

and James Kirby Martin—two historians whom I deeply respect—came up with the idea for this series, then, Franklin brought the concept to fruition. I'm proud to be a part of it, and thank them for the invitation to write the inaugural volume.

All mistakes, naturally, are my own.

Index

Decker's Ferry, 23
DeHart's Point, 22-23
Delaware River, xi
deserters, 4, 12, 16-17, 72
Dickinson, Philemon, 70, 89n16
Diemar, Friedrich, 59
Donop Regiment, 19, 43, 53, 59

Elizabeth River, 26-27, 53
Elizabethtown, 9, 11-12, 14-15, 18-
    19, 22-28, 33, 37, 40-43, 45-
    46, 49, 52-60, 72, 81n27,
    84n35
Elizabethtown Creek, 42
Elizabethtown Point, 14, 18-19, 22-
    23, 37, 41, 45, 49, 52, 54-56,
    59, 72, 81n27, 84n35

1st Connecticut Brigade, 6, 25
1st New Jersey Regiment, 10, 15, 28,
    35, 60
1st Pennsylvania Brigade, 6, 25
Ford, Jacob, xvii
Forman, David, 54
Forrest, Thomas, 61, 68-69
Fort Mercer, xi
Fort Mifflin, xi
Fort Ticonderoga, 68
Fort Washington, 2, 53
4th Continental Dragoons, 50
Franklin, William, 16-17, 48
Frederick the Great, 1
French and Indian War, 23

Galloping Hill Road, 19, 27-29, 35,
    37, 59-61, 70
Garrett Post House, 23
George III, 48
Gibbs, Caleb, 38, 40, 47, 50, 53
Gordon, William, 39
Governor's Island, 21-22
Green, Ashbel, 38-39, 42-43
Greene, Nathanael, xi, xviii, xxi, 5,
    38-39, 55, 57, 59-63, 68-76,
    87n7, 88n10, 89n16

Greenman, Jeremiah, 66, 88n10,
    88n13

Hachenberg, Carl Wilhelm von, 18-
    19, 37
Hamilton, Alexander, 25, 40-41, 43
Hand, Edward, 25, 39-43, 47, 50,
    84n35
Haverstraw Bay, 56
Heard, Nathaniel, 50-51, 87n5
Hills, John, 53
Hobart Gap, 18-19, 25, 27, 37, 60,
    63, 66, 71, 76, 87n7
Howe, Robert, 52-54, 72
Humphreys, David, 71, 88n10
Huntington, Jedediah, 10-11, 55
Huntington, Samuel, 16, 54
Hussars, 59

Iroquois Confederacy, 11
Irving, Washington, 67

Jäger Corps, 19, 23, 32, 34-35, 38,
    46, 53, 57, 59, 67, 69, 73,
    81n27, 82n5, 83n12, 85-
    86n8, 88n10, 89n22
Jelf's Hill, 24, 26, 28, 82-83n12
Jockey Hollow, xvii

Knox, George, 14
Knyphausen, Wilhelm von, xviii,
    xxiii, 1-2, 10, 12-13, 16-25,
    27-28, 32-43, 45-49, 51-53,
    55-63, 66, 69-74, 77, 79n1,
    81n26-27, 84n35, 86n2,
    86n13, 87-88n7, 88n10, 98

Lafayette, Marquis de, 3, 8, 38, 55
Landgraf Regiment, 18, 58
Lee, Henry "Light Horse Harry",
    xxi, 4, 16, 50, 53-55, 57, 59-
    60, 62-63, 66, 70-73, 86n13,
    87n7
Leib Regiment, 18, 24, 46, 59
Leslie, Alexander, 56